Visitors to China

Visitors to China

EYEWITNESS ACCOUNTS
OF CHINESE HISTORY

Keith L. Pratt

PRAEGER PUBLISHERS
New York · Washington

BOOKS THAT MATTER

Published in the United States of America in 1970
by Praeger Publishers, Inc.
111 Fourth Avenue, New York, N.Y. 10003

Library of Congress Catalog Card Number: 78–121717

Printed in the United States of America

To Sondra

Contents

Contents

List of Illustrations

FIGURES

MAPS

Acknowledgments

The author is most grateful to A. C. Barnes, Dr. Joseph Needham, and Edgar Snow for their helpful cooperation in the writing of this book; to Dr. Needham for permission to reproduce Figure 3; to Miss D. J. Paxton for the line drawing of Matteo Ricci and for Figures 9 and 10; and to the authors and publishers concerned for permission to quote from their works.

The publisher wishes to thank the following for their kind permission to reproduce the illustrations on the pages quoted: The British Museum, pp. 32 (plate 2), and 46, jacket illustration; J. Allan Cash, p. 38; The Gulbenkian Museum (Durham, England), pp. 32 (plate 3), 60; Hong Kong Government Information Services, p. 129; Hsinhua News Agency, p. 118; Royal Scottish Museum, Edinburgh, p. 13; The University of Durham (England), p. 48; The Wellcome Trustees, p. 61.

Introduction

In the year 1775 a book was published in the Poultry Yard, London, entitled *The Chinese Traveller*. According to the introduction, the aim of the work was to correct superficial accounts of China then being circulated through the publication of descriptions from certain Jesuit missionaries. Their names were given as du Halde, Lecomte, de Premare, "and others," and their observations were thought to be unbiased and discerning.

The intention of the book was admirable, for then as now there was a need to present the facts about China and its people on as firm authority as possible. Of the authors, only du Halde had not been to China, and he had collected in Paris so many fascinating reports from the men on the spot that in 1735 he was able to produce a monumental work, *Description . . . de la Chine*, in four volumes.

The editor of *The Chinese Traveller*, with commendable wisdom, stressed that a short tour did not provide sufficient experience on which to publish an informed description: "We must expect few useful or entertaining accounts from those who just touch upon the coast of the country, or dwell in it some time merely to trade there. . . . Their history of the manners, genius, and produce of a country will always be found defective, more especially as their education is limited to the branch of commerce, or to the profession which they pursue there." A similar charge can sometimes be leveled today against those who have but a brief acquaintance with the country and yet voice their opinions of it in public.

In execution, *The Chinese Traveller* fell only slightly short of its target. The eyewitness accounts were detailed and vividly written. The English reader could be left in no doubt as to the fallacy of imagining that tea, lacquered tables, pagodas, and respectful gentility were characteristics of Chinese society as a whole: Daily life for the majority was much more down to earth. On the other hand, personal experience did not give the Jesuits the understanding of Chinese history that could enable them to assess their observations in historical perspective. Neither did they have the modern critical approach to history, which is based on the use of original sources and, in particular, local records and is perhaps cautious of accepting official pronouncements at face value. This shortcoming, through no fault of their own, led them to produce the sort of generalization that was seized upon and believed by those Europeans for whom China was a model society, in preference to any amount of factual information. For example:

> Other states according to the common fate of things of this world, are sensible of the weakness of infancy; are born misshapen and imperfect; like men they owe their perfection and maturity to time. China seems more exempted from the common laws of nature; and as though God himself had founded their Empire, the plan of their government was not a whit less perfect in its cradle, than it is now after the experience and trial of four thousand years.

In fact, archaeology has so far revealed no evidence of organized administration as far back as the twenty-second century B.C.; neither would it be true to say that the practice of government in the eighteenth century A.D. was either efficient or particularly enlightened.

The problem facing the would-be reader of Chinese history is unfortunately much the same today as it was two hundred years ago. There is no lack of published material, but in the absence of expert advice how is he to assess its worth? Many books contain little more than generalizations, and others are written on the basis of a limited acquaintance with China and its history. Of the increasing number that do conform to the high standards expected of Western historical writing, few are intended for the beginner or general reader. More books are needed that will present the basic facts about Chinese civilization and on which further reading may be based.

It is important, when reading about contemporary China or speculating about the future course of Chinese affairs, to understand the historical background of this country, which is so different from any other. This book does not attempt to describe modern China in detail: it does attempt to put certain features of the Chinese way of life in historical perspective.

In the following chapters the theme of the Chinese traveler is brought up to date. The stories are told of a number of visitors who witnessed China in its great or significant periods. Their own accounts are used where possible, supplemented by other contemporary sources and the conclusions of modern research.

It may be possible to dispel some of the misconceptions that still exist about China. One of them is that its geographical position and its people's belief in their cultural supremacy caused it to indulge in a persistent and conscious policy of total isolationism, to shut itself off from the rest of the world

and to deny entry to foreigners. It was on this assumption
that some commentators in 1960 suggested that the sudden
departure of Russian technicians from China in that year
indicated a return to this policy. In 1966, the compulsory
closure of the last foreign mission school in China provoked
similar comment. While there is no doubting the Chinese
people's conviction of their own superiority, something that
has been acclaimed by writers from the beginning of the
Christian era to the present day, the following chapters will
show that China has not consistently refused entry to the
foreigner. Similarly, it has shown an interest in other parts of
the world, and some of its feats of exploration are as worthy
of study as those of the European discoverers.

Yet it must be said that the Chinese have never seen any
necessity to learn from the West. In the seventeenth century,
Matteo Ricci could say: "This nation measures all others
according to its own standards, and they are thoroughly con-
vinced that what is unknown to them is unknown to the rest
of the world." That a similar attitude prevails is today shown
by Dr. Joseph Needham, who writes:

> The libraries of western books in China are still very inade-
> quate, and although they reach such brilliant heights where
> their own culture is concerned, Chinese scholars in general, to
> say nothing of the broad Chinese public, really don't know
> enough about the rest of the world. Take Roman law and
> Greek philosophy for example. In all my wide acquaintance
> among Chinese intellectuals, I know of only two who are
> capable of reading Aristotle in the original Greek, and only one
> who knows anything about Justinian.[1]

The Opening Up of the West

In China support was usually denied to the section of society
that, in the Western world, provided the greatest incentive to

[1] Private communication to the author.

travel and exploration, the merchant class. Confucianism* regarded the merchant as unproductive and parasitic and trade
as a danger to the finely balanced agrarian economy. This is
not to say that trade was not practiced, even in the private
interests of members of the Confucian bureaucracy. But the
official justification of it was not the financial benefit of the
great industrialists or mercantile organizations; it was the attraction to China of goods with curiosity or luxury value.
From time to time, as in the Han (206 B.C.–A.D. 220) and
T'ang (618–907) periods, the demand of the court and upper
classes for foreign luxuries was considerable; in the T'ang
especially, many people made their living from the Indians
and Sogdians, the Persians and Arabs who thronged the
markets of China or came to present gifts at court. Yet in the
eyes of the administration these activities were not an essential
part of the national economy, nor could their encouragement
benefit it in any way. Permission to trade was a favor occasionally granted by the court to foreigners, which if forfeited
would damage their interests alone and not those of the
Chinese Empire.

   In a way, the Chinese were spoiled, for if merchants from
distant lands did not come to China themselves, there were
always plenty of Central Asian peoples willing to act as middlemen and carry Chinese goods away over the oceans or
deserts and mountains to India and farther west. The Chinese
themselves, when trading ambition did first lead them overseas,
were often discouraged by these same middlemen. Such was
the case of Kan Ying, who reached the head of the Persian
Gulf in A.D. 97. There he heard terrible stories from Parthian
sailors of the delays and sicknesses encountered to the west,
and he dared go no farther. The Parthians, of course, had
much to lose if the Chinese were to come into direct contact

---

* An asterisk indicates the first occurrence of a word to be found in the
Glossary.

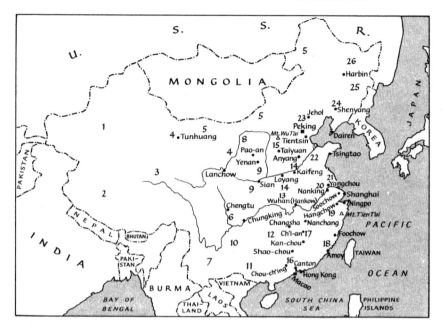

Map 1. The provinces of China and places mentioned in the text:

1 Sinkiang	8 Ninghsia	15 Shansi	21 Kiangsu
2 Tibet	9 Shensi	16 Kwangtung	22 Shantung
3 Chinghai (Tsinghai)	10 Kweichow	17 Kiangsi	23 Hopei
4 Kansu	11 Kwangsi	18 Fukien	24 Liaoning
5 Inner Mongolia	12 Hunan	19 Chekiang	25 Kirin
6 Szechwan	13 Hupeh	20 Anhui	26 Heilungchiang
7 Yunnan	14 Honan	(Anhwei)	

with the Roman Empire. They were making large profits from the section of the Silk Route that crossed their territory.

If commercial expansion was lacking as an organized incentive to exploration, three other factors were present in the early history of China that contributed greatly to the increase of its geographical knowledge, namely (1) military expeditions, (2) the growth of Buddhist* scholarship, and (3) the development of sea power.

(1) The extent of the Chinese Empire was pushed back to its natural frontiers during the early Han dynasty.* Efforts were then made to drive farther into Central Asia, originally as an attempt to solve once and for all the problem of recurring Hun raids on the northwest frontier, and subsequently to satisfy the ambitions of the court for power and prestige. In 138 B.C., an ambassador, Chang Ch'ien, was dispatched with orders from the Emperor* Han Wu-ti to make contact with the Yueh Chih. These were a people evicted from the Tarim Basin region by the Huns in 165 B.C., now believed to be reestablishing their settlements farther west.

Chang Ch'ien set out with a hundred men but was soon captured by the Huns, and it was ten years before he managed to escape and continue his mission. He took with him his wife, whom he had married during his captivity, and a Hunnish servant. Using information he had gathered from returning Hun scouts, he soon found the Yueh Chih. They, however, were now too concerned with plans for conquering Bactria* to become involved with the Huns, and after a year's stay in their country Chang Ch'ien was obliged to return to China to report the failure of his mission. On the way he was again captured, but a dispute over the Hun leadership gave him the chance of escaping.

The stories he told on his subsequent reception at court, particularly that of "heavenly, blood-sweating" horses, stimulated the curiosity of the Emperor. The Huns were defeated in 120 B.C., and fifteen years later an expedition was sent to the Yueh Chih to ask for specimens. Its members were murdered, and when a punitive force was also slaughtered in 104 B.C., the Han government found itself committed to full-scale military involvement beyond its frontiers. A force of sixty thousand soldiers, *corvée** laborers, convicts, and volunteers was sent out in 102 B.C. to extend Chinese control in the northwest and across the Tarim Basin.

For over a hundred years afterward, the Chinese Empire stretched like a huge finger into Central Asia, with military garrisons as far west as Yarkand. It is possible that the Egyptian geographer Ptolemy (A.D. 127–51) based the map of Asia in his "Guide to Geography" on the maps used by these outposts.

(2) Part of the significance of Chang Ch'ien's mission was its introduction of silk to peoples in contact with the Roman Empire. When the demand for this luxury increased in the West and caravans traveled frequently along the oases into China, Buddhist missionaries from India came with them.

The new faith reached China some time during the first century A.D. It spread rapidly and formed many sects. The supply of scriptures, however, was limited to the amount that could be transcribed by hand, for printing had not yet been invented. It was this shortage and the overused condition of the texts in his monastery library that persuaded one monk, Fa Hsien, to go on pilgrimage to India itself.

In A.D. 399 he and a number of companions left the capital and made for the northwestern border, where they intended to connect up with the regular caravan route. At the border town of Tunhuang they succeeded in joining the entourage of an official party and were given supplies by the Prefect, Li Hao. The prospect of the journey ahead of them, even in company, was frightening. Natural sources of food and water were scarce, the heat of the day was followed by extreme cold at night, sandstorms were frequent, and they were in constant danger of attack from mounted brigands. As Fa Hsien's later recollections show, the country too was forbidding: "The desert was full of evil spirits and hot winds which meant the death of anybody encountering them. Not a bird was to be seen in the sky, not an animal on the ground. When you looked around for landmarks, all you could see were the dry bones of earlier travelers who had perished."

However, the crossing of the desert was made in safety, and some two months after leaving Tunhuang the party reached Khotan. Fa Hsien was well received and was clearly impressed by the strength of the Buddhist Church. But it was not the goal the pilgrims had set out to attain, and they continued their journey. Eventually, having crossed a snow-capped mountain range where there were "poisonous dragons which . . . could produce storms of snow, sand or stones if provoked," they arrived in India. Here they were welcomed everywhere as the first Chinese Buddhists to be seen in this country and visited many monasteries and places of pilgrimage. Fa Hsien stayed in northern India for three years and learned to speak and write Sanskrit.* During this time he collected rolls of scriptures, which he packed up to take with him on the return journey to China in A.D. 411.

The merchant ship in which he sailed from the mouth of the Ganges took him first to Ceylon, which he found very attractive: "The weather," he wrote, "was so constantly warm and pleasant, and the trees so beautiful. Agriculture was carried on according to choice, and not at the dictation of the seasons." He stayed there for two years, until the sight of a merchant selling a white silk fan from China made him homesick. He had now been away from home for fourteen years and had lost contact with all his original companions.

He shipped out on a vessel with a complement of two hundred, which despite its size made heavy going of the voyage across the Bay of Bengal.

The sea was infested with pirates, whom to meet meant certain death. The boundless expanse of water spread out before us, the only aid to navigation being the sun, the moon and the stars.

If these were obscured by the weather the ship had to run unguided before the wind. At night great waves, shining like fire, broke against one another, and we caught glimpses of huge turtles and other sea monsters. The merchants were panic-stricken, not knowing where they were going, but it was impossible to drop anchor because the sea was so deep. . . . If we had hit a submerged rock there could have been no escape.

Fa Hsien spent much time in prayer.

When he did reach China, having spent five months in Java *en route*, he had been away for fifteen years. He estimated that he had visited thirty countries and could recount stories of others of which he had only heard. Even allowing for some natural exaggeration, Fa Hsien's journey was a great achievement.

(3) During the Sung dynasty (A.D. 960–1279), a number of factors combined to give the Chinese fleet mastery of the South China Sea and the Indian Ocean. First, natural disasters and crop failures caused a large population shift from north to southeast China, where the new inhabitants soon adopted the maritime customs of the seaboard areas. Second, the Chin invasion of north China in 1126 drove the Sung government into exile at Hangchow. When the Chin were in turn ousted by the Mongols, the Sung reviewed their military strategy. Ill-advisedly, they decided to attack the Mongols. The latter had already demonstrated their excellence in overland fighting, so Sung experts decided on a strategy based on command of the southern rivers and canals. A fleet was deployed to patrol not only the inland waterways but the coastline also. It failed to dislodge the Mongols, but the stimulus led to the introduction of revolutionary techniques in shipbuilding and navigation, one of which was the magnetic compass.

Third, the government relaxed its traditional objections to large-scale commerce and even offered assistance to merchants competing with the Muslims in India and Southeast Asia. The mutual advantage to be derived from cooperation between merchant and fighting fleets was appreciated. It was never assumed, however, that the primary function of shipping was to carry goods; it was, rather, to attack and defend. Imports continued to be regarded as tribute offered to the court by vassal states.

Under the Yuan and Ming dynasties the fleet grew, as did the number of tribute bearers coming to China by land and sea. In return, the Chinese presented gold, silver, silk and porcelain as tokens of favor. During the first three decades of the fifteenth century, seven great fleets were sent out on treasure-seeking expeditions. They numbered up to fifty transport vessels, including big treasure galleons, and were under the command of the eunuch* Cheng Ho. One of these fleets was to take home an ambassador from Melinda who had presented a giraffe for the Emperor of China's zoo, and it was this expedition that rediscovered the east coast of Africa in 1418. The original discovery, in the ninth century, had not been followed up because of a temporary wave of antiforeign feeling.

It was only the wildlife of Africa that seems to have impressed the Chinese. Fei Hsin, a member of the crew, wrote:

> The inhabitants live in solitary and dispersed villages. The walls are made of piled up bricks and the houses are masoned in high blocks. The customs are very simple. There grow neither herbs nor trees. Men and women wear their hair in rolls; when they go out they wear a linen hood. The mountains are uncultivated and the land is wide; it rains very rarely.

Chang Ch'ien, Kan Ying, Fa Hsien and Cheng Ho are not exceptional for the journeys they undertook. Descriptions of foreign lands by soldiers, diplomats, scholars, and traders of several periods exist and bear adequate testimony to the interest of the Chinese in the curiosities of the outer regions of the world. They were less concerned with foreign social conditions. For their part, Europeans visited China in increasing numbers after the sixteenth century and many spent their lives there. Books were written that related with admiration the customs, philosophies, and administrative system of China, as well as some of its strange sights. *The Chinese Traveller* was one such book, a partial attempt to satisfy the public interest with an accurate and objective description.

Further Reading

Jeanette Mirsky ed., *The Great Chinese Travelers* (New York: Pantheon, 1964) contains accounts by the Chinese of their own voyages of exploration. It includes the stories of Chang Ch'ien, Cheng Ho, and some nineteenth-century Chinese visitors to Europe. Fa Hsien's story is translated by H. A. Giles, *The Travels of Fa Hsien* (Cambridge, England: Cambridge University Press, 1923).

The most readable account of Chinese history is L. C. Goodrich, *A Short History of the Chinese People* (New York: Harper & Row, 1959). Michael Loewe, *Imperial China: The Historical Background to the Modern Age* (New York: Praeger, 1966) forms an excellent introduction to Chinese civilization, as does Derk Bodde, *China's Cultural Heritage: What and Whither?* (New York: Holt, Rinehart & Winston, 1957). A study of the help given by Westerners to Chinese people and their governments is Jonathan Spence, *To Change China: Western Advisers to China 1620–1960* (Boston: Little, Brown & Co., 1969).

Visitors to China

I

Shang Yang in the State of Ch'in

The earliest known ancestors of man in China lived in the Lower Palaeolithic period, some 500,000 years ago. Their remains were discovered in 1964 at Lantien in Shensi. They were, of course, ape-men, and the story of their evolution through the Mesolithic and Neolithic periods properly belongs to the study of prehistory. It is somewhere about 1500 B.C., as the Neolithic period is closing and the Bronze Age opening, that Chinese history begins. In other words, traces of civilized group organization discovered in China go back that far. Evidence suggesting an earlier dating may yet remain to be unearthed.

In 1500 B.C., the royal house of Shang ruled "China," which then consisted of only a few thousand square miles along the lower stretches of the Yellow River.* From 1384 B.C. onward, its capital was at Anyang. It was mainly an agricultural community, although growing numbers of clerks, astrologers, builders, and craftsmen indicate the beginning of other specialized occupations and a wider economy.

Map 2. The Warring States in 350 B.C.

In 1111 B.C.,[1] the Shang authorities were overthrown by
the inhabitants of the Wei River valley, who established the
Chou dynasty. For three hundred years, Chinese civilization
prospered under a feudal regime. But the kingdom was ex-
panding, and by the eighth century B.C. it was too large and
its communications were too poor for central authority to be
maintained. It split up into many states, which, despite their
continued feudal structure and professed allegiance to Chou,
were in practice totally independent.

As these states grew, the extent and influence of the Chou
domain were whittled away. There were 170 states in 722 B.C.,
and wars were frequent. By means of conquest and alliance,
the number had been narrowed to thirteen in 481. The most
important then were Ch'i, Chin, Ch'in, Ch'u, Wu, and Yueh.
After the middle of the fifth century, in the period known as
the Warring States, warfare became a full-time, tough profes-

[1] Various proposals have been put forward concerning the date of the
Chou conquest, ranging from 1122 to 1027 B.C. and including 1111 B.C.

sion. Previously it had been just one aspect of the feudal way of life, short battles conducted by noble lords according to strict rules. Now the battles and sieges stretched into months and even years, and nothing was barred. Peasants were conscripted. Some left their farms, forgot their local allegiances, and became mercenaries in neighboring states. Some went to offer tactical advice, some went as spies. The strength of armies increased to hundreds of thousands, and their leaders were qualified by skill and experience instead of by noble birth. For the sake of mobility over mountains and marshes, infantry replaced charioteers as the main fighting force. Cavalry divisions also appeared. Troops were armed with iron swords, lances and daggers, and some carried the new crossbow.[2]

Not everybody was intent on war, although most people experienced it and many made their living by it. Long after the collapse of real Chou rule, men were putting forward theories on how to restore it and bring the states together again. The earliest we know of is Confucius (*ca.* 551–*ca.* 479 B.C.). Other famous "philosophers," as they are usually called, were Mo Tzu (fifth century B.C.), Mencius and Chuang Tzu (fourth century) and Hsün Tzu (third century). They were all visionaries, for none of them had lived under a united empire and none could really imagine what unity would mean. Yet they urged the rulers of one state after another to give them a chance to put their theories into practice. Mostly they were not immediately successful, but the spread of their propaganda helped to make people in all states tire of continual warfare. Even if the rulers did not accept the details of the philosophers' reforms, they did accept their principle that there must be unification.

The story in this chapter is about one man to whom was

[2] Crossbows were first in prominence in Europe in the twelfth century A.D.

given the opportunity to make his ideas work. He was not, strictly speaking, a visitor to China, for in his day there was no China as such. But he was a visitor to the state of Ch'in, the state that conquered all other states and created the first Chinese empire just over one hundred years after his death. He was a politician, and it was his policies that helped Ch'in to achieve this.

His name was Yang Kung-sun, and he lived in the state of Wei in the late fourth century B.C. As a young man he read books on law and began his career in the state government. His talent was noticed by the Prime Minister, Tso Kung-shu, who, as he lay dying, recommended to the King that he should appoint Yang as a counselor. If he did not, Tso said, he should execute Yang to ensure that he would not sell his services to an alien government. The Prime Minister died, but King Hui rejected his advice on the grounds that Yang was too young for high responsibility. Yang did not wait to see whether he would heed the alternative suggestion. In 361 B.C., he fled westward into Ch'in.

The ruler of Ch'in, Duke Hsiao, wanted to extend his territory eastward to the Yellow River. Yang Kung-sun believed he could help, and a close friend of the Duke arranged an audience for him. Yang saw the Duke twice and talked about the ancient kings and emperors and how they had earned their reputations. The Duke went to sleep. Yang learned his lesson, and at his third interview he talked about the present, and how the Duke could make Ch'in great in his own lifetime. Their conversation lasted for several days, and this time Duke Hsiao was so fascinated that he did not notice that Yang had edged forward almost onto his own mat.

Yang proposed that the power of the Ch'in nobility in the provinces should be broken by the division of the whole state into *hsien*, or counties. These could be controlled directly from the capital. The central government would be staffed by military men and the laws tightened up. People would be rewarded for informing against each other. They would become so afraid of the law that lawlessness would be utterly stamped out. Then the greatness of Ch'in would be assured.

After further persuasion, Duke Hsiao let Yang put his reforms into practice. At first, people protested against the severity of the new laws. Then the Crown Prince himself was punished under one of them, and the opposition was stunned into silence. The local government and taxation systems were reorganized and weights and measures standardized throughout the state. Restrictions were placed on trade, and people were encouraged to grow more food. Agricultural expansion was the central pillar of Yang's program, for the livelihood of the whole people, the prosperity of the state, its attractiveness to immigrants, and its ability to defend its frontiers all depended on the efforts of the farmers.[3] "After five years," says the *Shih Chi*, "the people were rich and strong." In 343 B.C., the King of Chou gave Duke Hsiao the title of *po*, leader of all the state rulers.

In 352 B.C., Yang Kung-sun had been given a high military position, which he then justified by capturing two towns from his old state of Wei. Eleven years later, after Ch'i had seriously

---

[3] Despite the current emphasis on industrialization in China, the same remains as true today as it was in the fourth century B.C. Agriculture is still the basic industry, and if the harvest is bad the whole nation suffers. Much social kudos is given to the farmers in a community who produce the most food, and the government is spending heavily to overcome the traditional dependence on the weather. For instance, the soil of the North China Plain is very fertile, yet its harvests are rarely as abundant as they should be because of the erratic rate of flow of the Yellow River. This varies from a mere trickle in winter, when it has no use for irrigation purposes, to a torrent racing at 883,000 cu. ft. per second in summer, when it will often flood much of the Plain. In 1955, the government launched a building program of forty-six dams stretching from the Plain itself up to Lanchow in the mountains of Kansu. When these had become operational they were to have ensured a controlled flow of water all year around. Early in 1966, it was admitted that the departure of Russian technicians had caused the disruption of the scheme.

defeated it, Yang advised Duke Hsiao to invade Wei again
while it was still weak. Yang himself was put in charge of the
army, and the opposing Wei force was led by an old friend
of his, Prince Ying. When the sides came face to face, Yang
sent the Prince the following message: "We used to be friends,
and yet we are now generals in two different countries. How
can we possibly fight each other? I suggest we meet, have a
drink and some music, and come to an agreement for the
ending of hostilities. Then Ch'in and Wei can have peace."

The meeting was held and the agreement made, but as the
two leaders sat drinking afterwards, armed guards jumped
out and captured the Prince: It had been an ambush. Ch'in
soldiers fell upon the Wei army and routed it. Wei sued for
peace, King Hui regretting that he had let Yang go to Ch'in
so many years ago, and the territory as far east as the Yellow
River was ceded to Ch'in. Duke Hsiao rewarded Yang by
creating him Lord of the district of Shang and giving him
fifteen of its cities. He was then known as Shang Yang.

Two years later the Duke died. His successor, Prince Ch'in,
had had his nose cut off on Yang's orders, and in revenge he
now commanded Yang's immediate arrest for alleged con-
spiracy. Shang Yang fled into the mountains, but he was too
unpopular to find protection, and in any case his own laws
forbade people to harbor unauthorized travelers. He tried to
find refuge in Wei but was deported. Back in Shang, he
raised an army to defend himself. There was a battle and
Yang was killed. As a deterrent to would-be rebels, his body
was torn to pieces between chariots.

The Beginning of the Chinese Empire

Confucius and Mencius said that the states would unite voluntarily under a king and government of sufficiently high
moral caliber. Everybody would want to serve a really sincere

administration. Mo Tzu, too, accepted the idea that the ruler's personality was important, though he believed it was subsidiary to the main weapon of government, which was the law and its attendant system of rewards and punishments. But it was Shang Yang who provided Ch'in with the only political theory that could ever, in practice, have ended the feudal anarchy of the Warring States period.

His reforms made the law the impersonal ruler of the state. Once the law was established everybody, including the king, the nobility, and the politicians, was subject to it. It permitted no personal liberty, which might lead to criticism and rebellion. There could be no questions asked, no appeal, no leniency. People submitted because the authorities were strong and they were afraid of being found out. The penalties of the law were severe.

Shang Yang's philosophy, which is called Legalism, did not die with him in 338 B.C. Ch'in was building up its military strength. It could call on a million men to carry arms, and its arms included the deadly crossbow. It had had toughening experience against the barbarians to the west. It had skilled cavalry units. The politicians now knew that they also had the type of government that could enforce submission indefinitely once the military conquest had taken place. They could impose unification.

And they were right: No state could stop them. One by one, Ch'in defeated them all by a combination of military strength, fifth-column subversion, and control over water resources. Shang Yang anticipated the importance of this last when he laid plans for boosting agriculture. But in the Ch'in conquest water was not only harnessed to grow more food for the troops but also was channeled to provide them with transport. Furthermore, Ch'in underground agents broke dikes and flooded enemy crops or diverted streams to dry them up.

The last state, Ch'i, was annexed in 221 B.C., and the King of Ch'in took the title of the "First Emperor."

Directed by his Chief Minister, Li Ssu, the Emperor intensified the Legalist suppression of individual freedom. The law ordered exactly how everybody should live. It governed people's private lives: It stated, for example, what books they could read and how many children they could have. It governed their public lives: It called the men up to slave at mammoth building projects, roads, canals, and palaces for the Emperor. The biggest scheme of all was the Great Wall,* joining up and extending the existing walls along the northern frontiers of China. Millions of laborers died at this effort, either of starvation, of physical exhaustion, or under the whips of the guards. And the object of so much suffering? Perhaps it was to protect the new empire against invasion by the Huns of Central Asia; perhaps it was to keep the border Chinese in, and to ensure that they were not contaminated by non-Chinese ways; perhaps it was to break the spirit as well as the bodies of the Chinese manhood, so that it could not think of rebellion.

Inevitably they did rebel in time, but not until 209 B.C., shortly before the death of the Second Emperor. Living conditions had not improved under his rule. According to Ssu-ma Ch'ien, half of all the people to be seen on the roads had suffered corporal punishment, and every day there was a fresh pile of dead bodies in the marketplaces. The officials who executed the most victims were regarded as the most loyal to the government. The memory of Shang Yang was bitter.

The Chinese Script and Language

Li Ssu realized that so long as certain parts of the new empire were allowed to retain their strongly independent consciousness, it would be impossible to frame one administrative system that would apply to them all equally. For instance, the existence of different local weights and measures could cause enormous headaches to the central treasury when it came time to assess taxes or pay its officials, both of which it did in grain rather than in cash. Efficiency would depend on standardization; so too would the preservation of law and order. If southerners felt that regional distinctions were continuing in favor of northerners, they would cause trouble. There must be one center to which all Chinese could look for a standard ruling on every matter, and that center was established in the capital, Ch'ang-an.* A network of roads and canals was built, all leading in that direction and helping to focus attention on the seat of authority. Unfortunately for the Ch'in, the same roads also led the rebel armies to the capital in 206 b.c.

Perhaps the most important of Li Ssu's measures for standardization was the abolition of variations in the written script, giving all Chinese one system of writing. Imagine how inconvenient it would be if New Yorkers could read and write only in Old Gothic lettering and Texans only in copperplate. This was the sort of situation that existed in the new empire.

The earliest form of Chinese "writing" was probably pictographic. This means that instead of making up a shapeless word to convey the idea of an object, the scribe drew a picture of the object itself. The ancient Egyptians also "wrote" like this. No examples of the purely pictographic script exist today. We do not know exactly where in China it originated, nor how long it took to evolve into the script of the Shang dynasty. By that time many of the pictures had altered until they were hardly recognizable as pictures, and other symbols had been introduced that had no pictorial element. Only in a minority of cases was it still possible to recognize the meaning from the appearance. For example, Figure 1 *(a)* shows a left and a right foot on opposite sides of

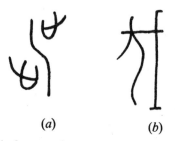

(a)   (b)

Figure 1. Oracle bone script

a stream, and meant "to cross"; Figure 1 *(b)* shows a man being struck in the neck with a dagger axe, and meant "to punish." We are fortunate that thousands of pieces of bone and shell, on which this type of writing was carved, have survived. They were used by court astrologers for keeping records and for answering questions about the future put to them by the King or the court. They are known as oracle bones, and the script as the oracle bone script.

During the early Chou period, a more formal style replaced the oracle bone script, and the pictographic element became more obscure. This was the Great Seal script, which had first been developed for making inscriptions on bronze. It looked like this: ✦ , to see; ✦ , a horse. It was this style that had degenerated and undergone changes in different parts of the country before Li Ssu brought everybody into line by insisting on the use of one comparatively simple version, the Small Seal (Fig. 2). The Great Seal and its variants were no longer used.

a vehicle   to see   the heart   a horse   an ear

Figure 2. Small seal characters and their modern forms

Plate 1. Oracle bones

Although Small Seal was easier to write than Great Seal, it was still more convenient for careful writing than for everyday use. For ordinary purposes another style, yet more simplified, became commonly used and in fact superseded Small Seal by the end of the Han dynasty. This was *li*, clerical script, and it is the style that has lasted almost unchanged in its printed form until the present day. It is written when particular neatness or clarity is required, but for general purposes the

Chinese use "grass" script. In this the characters are further simplified and the strokes joined together in the same way as we write English in longhand. A Chinese* can write a sentence in grass script as quickly as we can in English.

The printed script continues to be as important a unifying factor in China today as Li Ssu intended it to be in the third century B.C., for whereas all literate Chinese cannot understand each other's spoken dialects,* they can all read the same language in print. This is an important argument in favor of retaining the script and against the exclusive adoption of a phonetic style. Admittedly, the Chinese themselves find learning the characters a laborious process. However, the link with the past and the present link with other parts of the country are real advantages. To overcome the obvious disadvantage, a program of simplification in the printed clerical script is now under way.

As far as the written language itself is concerned, what changes there have been over the centuries have not been fundamental. The dual continuity of script and grammar over nearly two thousand years is most valuable to the Chinese historian, because it means he does not need to learn a "new" language to read documents even from as long ago as the Han dynasty. In this respect, he has an advantage over the Western historian, who must learn Anglo-Saxon, Middle English, or Old French to read primary sources of much less antiquity.

There is no Chinese alphabet. The written language consists of symbols, called characters. The *Chinese-English Dictionary*, by R. H. Mathews (Harvard University Press, 1966), lists some 15,000, which is far more than most Chinese can read. Nearly two thousand characters are essential for reading easier texts, and a sound working knowledge requires about twice that number.

To learn a Chinese character involves remembering (1) its appearance, (2) its pronunciation, and (3) its meaning.

Neither (2) nor (3) can be worked out from (1), so context is all-important when guessing at the meaning of a new character. Chinese children learn much of their vocabulary by parrot-like repetition from word lists.

The character is the equivalent of the English syllable, and words usually contain up to three syllables. It is rarely possible to translate one Chinese word with one English word, since the Chinese word often contains a number of implications. For example, we may speak of an "empty" room, but when the Chinese use the character 虛 , *hsü*, of a room, they imply that, besides being empty, it is also large, bright, and airy. We have no single word for this in English.

A character may also have more than one independent meaning. So, of course, may some English words, such as "well," "fine," "kind," and "fare." But the problem this raises for the translator of Chinese is more acute. The character 蕩 , *tang*, may be used in compounds to imply (1) vast, (2) dissipated, (3) smooth, (4) to destroy, (5) upset, (6) to clean up, (7) to drain, (8) a rocking movement. It was also the old name for a river in central China. Not many characters have as many as nine possible meanings, but most have more than one. The reader must decide from the context which is being used at any given time.

Furthermore, characters do not vary in appearance according to number, tense, or mood. Only the context can tell whether, for example, 書 , *shu*, means "book" or "books," or whether 吃 , *ch'ih*, means "eat," "eats," "eating," "will eat," "ate," or "eaten." Twentieth-century Chinese makes things clearer than the older language did, for there are now more grammatical particles.

Clearly, the difficulties to be faced in learning Chinese are not those encountered with Latin or German. Every language has its peculiar difficulties, and with Chinese it is the script. Spoken Chinese, at least in the Mandarin* dialect, is no more difficult than spoken French, and the younger one begins, the easier the task. Nor is the script itself insuperable, even for one speaking English. Those who make the effort will be richly rewarded, for Chinese literature is among the world's greatest.

Further Reading

A recent general survey of Chinese archaeology is by K. C. Chang, *The Archaeology of Ancient China*, rev. ed. (New Haven: Yale University Press, 1968).

The description of the career of Shang Yang is taken from his biography in the *Shih Chi* (ch. 68), *The Book of the Lord Shang* translated by J. J. L. Duyvendak (Chicago: University of Chicago Press, 1963).

2

Romans in Han China

The people of the new empire quickly acquired a national spirit. Theirs, they said, was the greatest country in the world. People beyond China with any pretense to civilization or culture must have derived it from contacts with the Chinese. The farther away from China they lived, the more barbarous they became. On the other side of the world, the Romans were thinking much the same about their empire. They had heard something about the Chinese, just as the latter at least knew of the existence of Rome, but neither side appreciated the extent or importance of the other.

The Ch'in dynasty fell to the Han, whose influence spread into Central Asia. States from Korea to Ferghana* sent presents, pledging their allegiance in return for military protection. The court welcomed their tribute and wallowed luxuriously in its reputation. Most of the gifts consisted of local products from the areas concerned, such as ivory, precious stones, or animal skins, and were chosen for their attractiveness or curiosity value.

In A.D. 120, an embassy reached the capital, Loyang, from the kingdom of Shan. It had something extra and spectacular to offer, a group of traveling players. The official history of the later Han, *Hou Han Shu,* describes their act. It mentions conjuring, firespitting, juggling, and some kind of contortionist feat, which gave the impression that the performers could cut off their arms and legs and assume the head of an ox or horse. Some of the players were musicians, and they all took part in the New Year celebrations at court. Emperor An-ti was well pleased.

What matters to us is not the show itself, though stories like this give life to history, but the fact that the artists came from Roman Syria. They must have been adventurers as well as entertainers, for they are the first known Romans to have ventured beyond India. The beginning of their story, of how they crossed the Bay of Bengal and reached Shan, in modern Burma, can only be conjectured. Neither do we know whether they so impressed the King that he invited them to join the mission to China, or whether they were taken unwillingly as slaves. In either case, they accompanied the Shan officials up the Salwin river. It was a dangerous route, not often used, over rough mountains and torrential rivers.

Eventually they found themselves in the Chinese province of Shu, which was, and still is, one of the most beautiful places on earth. Today it is called the Red Basin of Szechwan. To the Romans the rolling plain ringed with mountains, the subtropical trees and foliage, the birds and butterflies, and the gentleness of the climate even in winter must have made it a dream come true. The fields were full of wheat, fruit, and vegetables: This was the main food-growing area for the "home counties" around Loyang. If they were observant, and if they knew anything of agriculture in the West, the Romans might have noticed equipment and techniques new to them, such as cast-iron plows for deep furrowing and breast-strap harness on the horses (Fig. 3). The ordinary farmer could not afford such aids, but the tenant farmer, who had given up some of his freedom to rent land on a private estate, might have them as compensation. Landlords sometimes provided new machinery and took an interest in agricultural developments. They tried crop rotation, big irrigation schemes, and the planting of new roots and seeds such as celery, onions, garlic, melons, and clover.

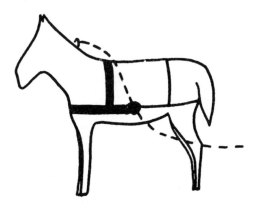

Figure 3. Breast-strap harness

The Shan party came first to the regional capital, also called Shu. The Romans must have been amazed at its size and life, for it was one of the largest towns in the empire. It was a busy receiving and dispatching point for both country produce and local salt, copper, gold, and silver. It had lacquer* and weaving industries. In short, it gave the impression of general prosperity and was in fact the home of several millionaires.

In such pleasant surroundings, appearances were deceptive. Most of the common people, dressed in their regulation blue or green serge, were hopelessly poor. They could own their own farms as free men, but it was often impossible to do so and pay the taxes involved. When starvation threatened, some

turned to banditry; some left their homes, registered as dis-
placed persons, and qualified for government aid; some, by
far the majority, moved on to rented land. By submitting to
the control of the landlord, they surrendered much of their
families' freedom of action in return for exemption from taxation. Unfortunately, the great landowners often turned out
to be cruel and greedy, and then the rents ended up even
higher than the taxes. The people, naturally, complained.
Some of their grievances found their way into books and have
survived. Ts'ui Shih (A.D. 147–68) emphasized that things
became no easier even for those who chose servitude: "When
the harvest is bad they drift about and starve in ditches; they
marry off their wives and sell their sons" (*Political Commentary*). The cry of the poor, oppressed by the rich, is repeated
frequently in subsequent dynasties.

The Shan mission was taken from Shu to Loyang. Here
there were more obvious signs of the deep gulf between the
upper and lower classes. In theory, the distinction was based
not on wealth but on education and position. Government
workers constituted the greater part of the upper class. Many
were exempt from taxation and from the *corvée*, which
sometimes brought hardship to farms and other households
dependent on their menfolk. Their privileges were protected
by the law, and they were shown the utmost respect by the
rest of society. Until the twentieth century, the highest
achievement imaginable by most villagers was to obtain even
a minor official post.

The lower class consisted of scholars without government
posts, farmers, factory workers, and self-employed craftsmen,
soldiers, and merchants. Of these, the farmers were hailed as
the backbone of the state, though they received little reward
for it. The merchants did nothing to feed hungry mouths, so
their activities were restricted, as they had been ever since the
Chou dynasty. Under the Han they paid extra taxes, were not

allowed to use carriages or horses, and could not wear silk. These regulations were not, however, damaging, even when they were enforced: Officials relied heavily on the merchants to fill their homes with luxuries.

There was still one other class, called by the Chinese *chien min*, or "despicable people." These were the slaves, prostitutes, entertainers, and beggars, and their status was usually heredi-tary. Freedom could be granted only by their owners, if any, or by the government. They had no rights, though the law did protect them from inhuman punishments, such as burning.

The state, that is, the educated people in charge of govern-ment departments, insisted that class distinctions should be observed. Nevertheless, theory and practice did not entirely correspond. Take, for example, this description of China in the late second century A.D. by Chung-ch'ang T'ang: "The mansions of the great landowners stretch in rows by the hundred. . . . Dealers and merchants move about in their boats and carts in all directions. . . . The grandest houses are not big enough to contain all their jewelry and gems; the hills and valleys are not wide enough to contain all the horses, oxen, sheep and pigs." Here we see that, although society is divided, it is not only into the educated and uneducated but also into the "haves" and "have-nots." Traders are still criticized for being uneducated and unproductive, but they are as wealthy as anybody—the landowners, the industrialists, even the nobility.

As the theory of class broke down, so did some of the laws upholding it: Craftsmens' wives put on the jade* and silver brooches made by their husbands, which only the top people were really allowed to wear; merchants ordered silk clothes for themselves, and if the law caught them at it, they would either thumb their noses, perhaps by dressing their servants in silk, or bribe the officials to look the other way.

In A.D. 120, when the Romans came to Loyang, even the

principle that government posts went only to the best qualified applicants was not observed. The educational system was
in a temporary state of collapse: The grounds of the Imperial
Academy* had been turned into a vegetable garden. Money
and influence bought political power. Rich families, such as
the Liangs, the Wangs, the Ts'aos, and the Tengs, now exerted control through their jobs, as well as their houses and
estates. They competed with the merchants in the size of their
houses, the number of servants, their reputations as hosts.
The upper class was more distinguishable by wealth than by
breeding. Genuine scholars began to leave the government
in protest against its laxity and overindulgence.

The signs were there, but as yet there was no serious challenge to the authority of the dynasty. Many officials continued
to work conscientiously. Let us take the example of Chang
Hao, Commandant of Justice, whom the Romans might have
passed in the streets of Loyang. He is an important government minister, part of whose job is to advise local authorities
on the use of punishments and to act as adjudicator in dubious
court cases. His offices occupy a five-story building in the
center of the city. They are sparingly furnished. Chairs and
tables are as yet unknown, and wooden platforms covered in
damask serve as both. Legal documents on bamboo,* wood,
and silk are stacked along the walls. Like most officials, Chang
is expected to spend four successive nights in the office, so
in one room is his bed. It is really no different from his seating
accommodation, except that it has a wooden pillow. It is not
as grand as the beds in his own house, which are four-posters
with curtains to conceal the occupant and cotton sheets.

Chang is given one day off in every five, when he is expected to go home to his family and to bathe and wash his
hair. His house is at the south end of Loyang, just inside the
main gates of the city. It is a three-story, half-timbered building, brightly painted and with a curved roof. There are two

courtyards in the front, surrounded by high walls and connected by a gate in the middle. Willows and almond trees have been planted to throw shade onto the balcony at the front of the house. There is an outside staircase, and most of the living rooms are upstairs. In summer, they are cool and dark after the bright sunlight outside, for the eaves of the roof overhang, and there are woven blinds to keep out the heat and the flies. The servants occupy the outbuildings on either side of the main courtyard.

The house has an air of quiet luxury about it. In the main hall, the silk tapestries are the best from Shantung. The floor is covered with an expensive Kashmir carpet, and the ornaments, one of them a plaster head from India, are tastefully arranged on pedestals. In one corner stands an ornate bronze lampholder. Nearby, somebody has left a *p'i p'a,** the new instrument from the Western Regions,* which was used last night after dinner. The Changs had invited thirty guests. It was against the law to have so many, but who was to question the Commandant of Justice? They had dined on shellfish, ants' eggs, tortoise, pork, veal, onions, celery, turnips, and rice. It had been a small but good meal, rounded off by lychees and tangerines from Shu and washed down with rice wine. Late in the night, people had defied the curfew to watch the drunken guests leave in their carriages.

On the following morning, Chang returns to his office. His hair is tied up under his hat, which is decorated with two horns. These symbolize the sacred ram, which can tell right from wrong. He wears a loose-fitting, embroidered robe with wide sleeves, tied with a silk girdle, and leather shoes covered in lacquer. A sword hangs by his side. The servants harness two horses to the carriage and arrange the scarlet screens and black silk cover to which his rank entitles him. Outside in the street, traffic is heavy and progress slow. Chang listens to his outrider clearing a way through the pedestrians and shouting back at some unemployed laborers as they fling insults. He knows that none would actually dare to touch the carriage for fear of a serious court charge.

Eventually the office is reached and Chang begins work. He has before him a report from the Prefect of Hung-nung in Honan Province, with a request for advice. It concerns the case of a youth of sixteen, brought before him by his father as being beyond parental control. The boy refused to observe the mourning* period after his grandfather's death, came to blows with his father about it, and finally left home. He was then arrested and taken before the Prefect. In a case brought by a parent against one of his own family, no witnesses were required, and after being caned the boy admitted his guilt. For striking his father the penalty was death. In this case, however, the father was pleading for leniency. He himself has suggested exile as a punishment, and the Prefect has referred to Chang Hao before making a final decision. Chang studies the report carefully. Finally he commends the father's sympathy for his son, and approves the suggestion that he be sent to an army unit in the Western Regions.

Han Law

Although many of its details have changed, the law on which Chang Hao was an expert has served ever since as the basis of the Chinese legal code. Some of its provisions seem harsh by our standards, but so do those of nineteenth-century England. Some seem illogical: for instance, a man could die merely for disobeying his father, yet he was permitted to kill anybody he found trespassing on his property after dark. Circumstances, of course, decide and alter cases. Who is to say that in two thousand years' time, historians will not regard as illogical some aspects of twentieth-century law that seem perfectly reasonable to us?

The death penalty was carried out either by decapitation or by cutting the body in two at the waist. Burning and boiling as means of execution hardly ever occurred. For more serious offenses, the head of the mutilated corpse was exhibited in the marketplace, which brought extra shame to the victim's family. In extreme cases the criminal's parents, paternal grandparents, wife, children, brothers, and sisters were also punished.

The next most severe punishment was hard labor. Terms ranged from one to five years. Although the maximum sentence was not a long time compared with current Western practice, to Han convicts it was a fate worse than death. Their heads were shaven, they wore iron collars and leg irons, and they were beaten by the guards as they struggled at their work. Usually they built walls or roads. They might also suffer physical mutilation, either by castration, tattooing, or the loss of nose, hands, or feet. This form of punishment was abolished in 167 B.C. Castration, which had been abolished earlier, was later reintroduced and abolished again in A.D. 81. Further occurrences of mutilation are found in the Later Han, but by this time the most common form of corporal punishment was the bastinado.*

The law was more lenient to imperial clansmen* and members of the nobility. If, for example, they were found guilty of a crime which normally carried a mutilating punishment, they might only be sentenced to collect firewood. This was not just a technicality that meant they were being pardoned. For a member of the nobility to have to perform such a menial task would involve great shame and loss of dignity, and this was real punishment in Han society. Certain high officials were also adjudged to be above the workings of the ordinary criminal law, and the emperor himself had to approve any sentence passed on them. When the penalty was death, the emperor might graciously permit the unfortunate victim to commit suicide rather than have to submit to the scandal of public execution.

If the law was hard, it was not as cruel as it had been during the Ch'in dynasty. Han law had its humane side. The convicted criminal could appeal within three months, and if his sentence was to more than two years' hard labor his relatives could also appeal. In this way the state gave some protection to the breadwinner of the family. It also considered its other members: Family allowances were made in the form of grain issues and tax relief; members over eighty were given pensions of grain, meat, wine, or cloth; the very young and the very old could be prosecuted only in exceptional circumstances.

Occasional pieces of legislation also show a concern for everyday affairs. From time to time, relief was offered to people breeding horses for the government; a woman's dowry was to be returned if she was divorced; rewards were offered for killing tigers; hunting for birds' nests was forbidden in spring and summer; guards were fined for not dismounting at the palace gates.

At the beginning of the Christian era, this was the most comprehensive and best organized legal system in the world. In its control over peoples' lives, it might be compared with that of any modern state.

The Silk Trade

Forty years after the Syrian players had been to Loyang, Roman merchants reached the southwest frontier of China and made the first direct trading link between the two empires. This was not their first commercial experience of each other. Back in the second century B.C., Eastern goods had seeped through to the West, and a regular demand was set up in the first century when Chinese encampments were less than 1,500 miles from the Roman borders. Except for one battle in 36

B.C., when 150 Roman mercenaries helped to defend a city in Sogdiana* against the Chinese, the two sides never came into contact personally. It was principally the Parthians who saw to that, for they made a profit out of carrying goods from one to the other. Though their prices were high, the commercial ambition of Gaius Gracchus and Augustus and the desire of the Chinese court for fame and pleasure outweighed the expense. Trade was conducted on a more or less regular footing between one side of the world and the other.

It was the Romans who needed the trade most. The Chinese derived little from it except luxury goods: Glassware, small sculptures, coral, rugs and embroideries. The fact that these might have come from the Roman Empire meant nothing to them; they could obtain equally interesting trinkets from a dozen places. In fact, the original Roman payment for their Chinese imports usually failed to arrive, goods from India or the Central Asian states being substituted *en route*. The Chinese were none the wiser and really did not care, so long as their luxuries arrived from somewhere.

The Romans, on the other hand, developed a craving for silk that could not be satisfied. It spread to all parts of the empire, including Britain, and to all sections of society. There were other valuable imports, such as pepper from India and ivory from Africa, but silk was the most essential. Silk came only from China, from the people known to the Romans as the Seres, so it was imperative that trade with China should be maintained.

The silk came in bales, either as woven cloth or as raw yarn. Each bale was marked with its place of origin, dimensions, and value. Raw silk was taken to one of the Syrian processing centers, of which the most famous was at Tyre. There the roll was ungummed and the fibre unwound before being made up into material form. The Roman weave was very fine. Some cloth was even re-exported to China.

Early in the first century A.D., the pattern of trade changed. Previously the main routes from West to East had been overland, from Syria to Seleucia, across the Persian desert to Merv, and into China by way of its Central Asian dependencies. Roman hostility to Parthia and the profiteering ambitions

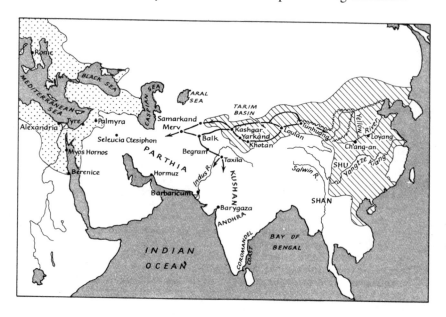

Map 3. The farthest extent of the Han (striped area) *and Roman* (dotted area) *empires and some of the main Central Asian trade routes* (arrows)

of the middlemen made this arrangement unsatisfactory. Alternative routes were tried without much improvement. Then, in 50 B.C., Egypt was annexed as a Roman province, and Roman sea power along the Red Sea coastline increased. The discovery by a man named Hippalus that monsoon winds could be used to blow ships over the open sea to the west coast of India was popularized. Traders there were already dealing with China. To adopt this route meant exchanging one lot of agents for another, but the Indians appeared to be fair-minded and eager to trade on their own account. Their customs duties and transit fees were not too heavy. By the end of the first century, the old overland route had fallen into disuse.

The sea link with India was well used. The historian Strabo tells of 120 vessels that left just one of the Red Sea ports, Myos Hormos, for the East each summer. For those lucky enough to complete it, the voyage took a little over one month. All sailors faced perils enough from storms and ship-wreck; those who hugged the coast around the Arabian Peninsula also needed archers as defense against pirates.

Ships with cargoes for China headed for the Kushan ports of Barbaricum and Barygaza, which had specialized docking, unloading, and storage facilities. At Barygaza they sometimes found a queue of ships, waiting either for pilots to see them in through the narrow tidal channels or for a berth to be vacated by one of the larger Indian vessels sailing for the east coast. It was rare for a Roman sailor to venture farther than the Coromandel coast, although the Indians regularly crossed the Bay of Bengal to Southeast Asia.

At Barbaricum and Barygaza the ships were unloaded. The goods should then have been put onto caravans for transporta-tion to China by way of Taxila and Balk. However, the greater part of the cargoes consisted of gold and silver, in either cash or bullion. This the Indians retained for themselves, loading local products onto riverboats and pack animals. The Chinese were unaware that any substitution had taken place, while in India vast hoards of Roman coinage were accumu-lated.

The silk trade flourished for over 200 years. So much gold and silver was drained from the Roman Empire that there was insufficient to continue minting in the earlier proportions, and the real value of the currency fell. Indian collectors then became less anxious to acquire it and consequently needed more persuasion to act as middlemen. Some Romans bypassed them and reached southern China for themselves. Chinese sources mention two groups in particular, one in A.D. 226 and another some sixty years later. But toward the end of the third century, Roman sea power was in decline, and Persian fleets competed for control of the Indian Ocean. Contacts with the East became increasingly difficult.

At the same time, Chinese export arrangements wavered. The collapse of the Han dynasty, in A.D. 220, was followed by a period of political and economic instability. Some merchandise did continue to trickle through to the West: Ammianus Marcellinus saw some at the Batanea fair on the Euphrates in 360. In 552, however, Europe obtained the silkworm for itself, and links between the Mediterranean and China were temporarily discontinued.

Further Reading

There are three major sources of information about the Han dynasty. Sections of Ssu-ma Ch'ien's *Shih Chi*, which covers the period before 100 B.C., have been translated by Burton Watson, *Records of the Grand Historian of China* (New York: Columbia University Press, 1961), and E. Chavannes, *Mémoires Historiques de Se-ma Ts'ien* (Paris, 1895). The official histories of the dynasty, the *Han Shu* (206 B.C.–A.D. 24) and the *Hou Han Shu* (A.D. 25–220) remain to be translated in full, as do the official histories of all later dynasties. Parts of the *Han Shu* are translated by H. H. Dubs in Pan Ku, *History of the Former Han Dynasty, Vol. 1* (New York: American Council of Learned Societies, 1938). Michael Loewe, *Everyday Life in Early Imperial China* (New York: Putnam, 1968) is an interesting reconstruction of early Han society.

3

A Japanese in T'ang China

The successors of the Han were unable to recapture its power and glory, and several shorter, less capable dynasties brought foreign invasion and division of the country. The period between A.D. 220 and 589, when China was reunited, cannot be dismissed as insignificant. It witnessed important developments in literature and the arts and was the time when Buddhism spread most rapidly and took on distinctive Chinese forms. However, the achievements of those years are most easily seen as part of the inheritance of China's greatest dynasty, the T'ang.

From the seventh century onward, merchants and diplomats alike were attracted from all over Asia by the stories of the glorious T'ang Empire. Its capital, Ch'ang-an, and its large ports became cosmopolitan centers where a Japanese might rub shoulders with Persians or an Indian with Jews as the crowds jostled in the streets and markets. Pilgrims and scholars came too, as China superseded India as the center of the Buddhist world. Their destinations were often the rich li-

braries of Ch'ang-an or the monasteries of the two holy
regions, Mount T'ien T'ai in the southeast and Mount Wu
T'ai in the north.

*Plate 2. A T'ang dynasty mini-
ature of a bullock cart*

*Plate 3. A cast-iron horse of the
T'ang dynasty. Height (to top
of head): 21 inches*

   In July, 838, two Japanese monks, Ennin and his student
Ensai, set out to make the journey to T'ien T'ai. They had
been given titles as part of an official mission to the Chinese
court and intended to visit the mountain while the Japanese
ambassador was in Ch'ang-an. The three ships made two
unsuccessful attempts to pass the rocks at the tip of the Japanese archipelago, until at the third try the wind had veered
north of east and carried the fleet in the direction of China.
There was little the crews could do to influence their course:
They checked their progress by the heavens and prayed for
safety. After six days, Ennin's ship ran aground on a sandbank,
and a rescue party revealed that they had reached the mainland near the mouth of the Yangtze* river.

The Japanese hired two boats to take them by canal to the nearby center of Yangchow, where they could make their arrival known to the Chinese officials. The canal teemed with craft of all sorts and sizes. Yangchow was a lively and rich town. It was the administrative center of the southeast and the headquarters of banks, government departments and industries. It had several shipyards and was the key point in the national canal network. Here grain, salt, tea, and other products were loaded onto long lines of barges for shipment to the north; so too were medicines, spices, rare woods, and other foreign luxury goods brought up from the great port of Canton; so too were the taxes collected from the Yangtze provinces. Convoys for the latter carried armed guards, yet only a part of the original consignment ever seemed to reach the capital.

The Japanese applied for permission to continue their journey, the ambassador's party to Ch'ang-an and the two monks and their servants to T'ien T'ai. Their request had to be relayed to the capital and the wheels of officialdom were numerous and slow. While they waited, Ennin and Ensai were lodged at the town's official monastery and the government hotel. The delay was not unpleasant, for Yangchow was a beautiful town and could provide sights and entertainment in plenty. When travel documents did eventually arrive, Ensai was to be allowed to go to T'ien T'ai and to stay there as a student; Ennin, however, had to return to Japan with the ambassador the following year, and it was not considered worth his while to go south for so short a time.

When the ambassador returned to the southeast at the end of March, 839, after his audience with the Emperor, Ennin did in fact take ship again. But he had not given up hope of fulfilling his original intention. When the vessels had left their last anchorage on the Shantung Peninsula and were heading back for Japan, Ennin's absence was discovered. He had been given shelter by some Korean monks in a small monastery, and here he spent the winter of 839, carefully watched by the local officials.

On the advice of the Koreans, Ennin now decided to make Mount Wu T'ai the object of his pilgrimage. The Chinese had been presented with something of a *fait accompli* as far as Ennin's continued presence was concerned, and the next spring they gave him permission to begin his journey. For a week or two his progress was frequently held up while his documents were renewed, for in that province no administrative area could issue credentials to travel beyond its jurisdiction: The county could authorize passage only as far as the prefecture, the prefecture as far as the provincial capital. Ennin was generally well entertained and showed no sign of impatience.

When they were allowed to continue, he and his companions found walking no difficulty. Before the rebellions in 755 and 780, the government had provided good roads, bridges, and ferries, and these were still maintained. As they crossed the North China Plain the party slept in monasteries whenever possible or, alternatively, in one of the many inns. Occasionally they begged hospitality from private householders, whose food was not always as good as Ennin expected and who did not always make the pilgrims welcome. Most of the people on the plain were poor. The government had lost control of certain areas, especially in the north, and landlords and officials were unscrupulous about extorting high rents and illegal taxes. Flood, drought, and pests frequently ruined the peasants' crops. This is how the T'ang writer Lu Chih (754–824) described their life: "All the year round they work themselves to death without a day's rest and when they have paid all their debts they live in constant anxiety whether they will be able to make both ends meet." Ennin himself saw human beings living on cattle fodder.

The travelers themselves sometimes went hungry, but they suffered no serious effects. On the evening of their arrival at the T'ing Tien cloister in the Wu T'ai region, Ennin recorded in his diary: "Leaving aside rest days, we have been on the road exactly forty-four days and fortunately have been entirely free of illness on the way" (June 3, 840).

Moving among the monasteries on the holy peaks, Ennin played a full part in the busy life of the communities. His diary shows that in addition to working in the libraries, he attended ceremonies, feasts, and lectures; went on excursions to shrines and places of interest; and had interviews with leading churchmen. He was not by any means the only visitor, for in the early ninth century Buddhism was an important element in the life of the people, and laity as well as visiting clergy attended functions on Wu T'ai. The setting was perfect: The grandeur of the mountain peaks vied for Ennin's praise with the delicacy of the wild flowers; the wooden buildings were brightly painted and ornately carved; inside were banners, lanterns, bells, vessels, and the statues of the Buddhas* themselves, all richly decorated with gold and jewels; and then there was the sound and color of the ritual. Little wonder that the peasants turned to Buddhism for some consolation in their hard lives, and little wonder that the government envied the church its growing support.

Ennin stayed on Wu T'ai for two months. By then he had completed work on the texts in the libraries, and on August 2, 840, he set off for Ch'ang-an in search of further instruction. The Chinese monks who accompanied him showed him the sights. One excursion in particular impressed Ennin: "We went together out of the west gate (of Taiyuan) and went three or four *li** west to a rocky mountain called Chin Shan. There is coal all over the mountain, and all the people from prefectures near and far come and get it to burn. For cooking meals it has a great amount of heat."

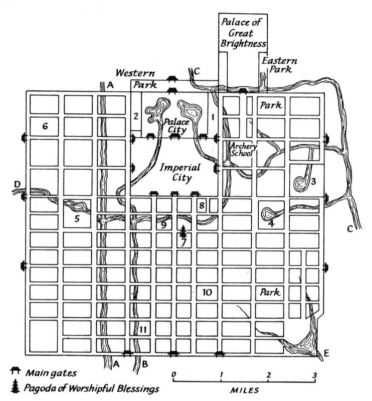

Map 4. The elaborate walled city of Ch'ang-an in the T'ang dynasty

KEY: 1 Eastern palace   6 Site of Han dynasty
      2 Side apartments   university
      3 Palace of Prosperous   7 An Jen ward
         Blessings   8 Jail •
      4 Eastern market   9 Courier rest post
      5 Western market   10 Military command post
                                      11 Park

         A Eternal Peace Canal
         B Clear and Shining Canal
         C Dragon's Head Canal
         D Transport Canal
         E Yellow Canal

Ennin reached the capital on September 21 and registered as a foreign student. He was given a room in the Paradise Cloister, in the An Jen (Quiet Understanding) quarter, and settled into a routine of research work, lectures, and services in the city's monasteries. The quiet of the Buddhist halls contrasted with the noise outside. Nearly a million people lived within its walls, slightly more than in the whole of England. It was probably the greatest city in the world. Among its amenities were shops, markets and warehouses, offices and hotels, schools, libraries, and scores of monasteries, some with pagodas that soared high into the sky. People thronged the streets and parks and canals. Those from the slum areas feasted their eyes on the fine clothes of the rich; rich and poor alike stared at the colorful processions of foreign diplomats moving toward the imperial* palace from their quarters, carrying exotic gifts.

The An Jen ward was near the center of the city. It is unlikely that Ennin was not caught up to some extent in its daily life, yet his diary gives little information about this. Perhaps he was too absorbed in his studies, or perhaps he was preoccupied with the ominous restrictions Emperor Wu-tsung was placing on Buddhist activities. In the light of historical perspective the years 842–45, during which Ennin was in Ch'ang-an, are seen as the time of the greatest religious persecution in Chinese history. After initially patronizing Buddhism, the Emperor had then turned to Taoism* and finally issued a series of orders defrocking virtually all Buddhist clergy. Ennin ruefully recorded this and other measures for the destruction of buildings and the confiscation of their contents. He became personally involved in June, 845, when all foreign monks in Ch'ang-an were ordered to leave the country. As he made his way towards Yangchow and the sea again, he passed through regions still loyal to the government and saw how thorough the administration had been: The

Plate 4. The Great Wild Goose Pagoda in Ch'ang-an, climbed by Ennin on March 9, A.D. 841

persecution, he recorded, was as complete in the provinces as it had been in the capital. Thousands of clergy had been turned homeless and penniless into the countryside, monasteries had been stripped of their wealth and demolished, scriptures had been destroyed.

Ennin himself continued to be politely, even warmly, received by officials. Shortly after Wu-tsung's death in April, 846, his successor proclaimed an amnesty. By this time, however, there was little left to attract Ennin back to the capital. After spending a year with his friends the Koreans in Shantung, he left for home on October 14, 847.

The Three Religions

China has sometimes been called the "land of three religions," Confucianism, Taoism, and Buddhism. Of these, only the first two were purely Chinese teachings. Buddhism came to China during the Han dynasty. As its Sanskrit scriptures were translated into Chinese terminology, its basic philosophical concepts were adapted to suit the more material Chinese attitude to life and religion. A number of Chinese sects originated, one of which is widespread in the West today under its Japanese name of Zen. In China it was called Ch'an. Some of these sects maintained a deeply spiritual existence in isolation from the outside world. But to the ordinary people, especially in the T'ang period, Buddhism meant images, ritual, and intercessions to the Buddhas and Bodhisattvas,* and this was very different from the individual and comtemplative nature of Indian Buddhism.

Buddhist scholarship in China reached its peak in the fourth and fifth centuries. Indian missionaries and Chinese converts performed monumental feats of translation and still found time to produce many original works, explaining doctrine and answering their critics. The highest point of Buddhist numerical strength came somewhat later, probably around the year 842, for which a total of 44,600 monastic houses has been recorded. The riches of the monasteries, at a time when the national treasury was in a bad way, was one incentive to Emperor Wu-tsung to curtail their activities. The persecution of 842–45 dealt Buddhism a blow from which it never fully recovered.

From the Han dynasty on, Taoism was debased in popular

practice, as Buddhism was later on, by its association with a multitude of gods and superstitions. Pure Taoism was the philosophy of the *Lao Tzu* and *Chuang Tzu*. In every object, they said, there is a Moving Spirit, *Tao*. This Spirit forms the object, dwells in it and gives it its nature and appearance. Although it is in all things, the Spirit is One. It is the originator and controller of the Universe. The human being can appreciate and associate himself with the Spirit by contemplation and the observation of Nature. It gives him complete contentment.

Some found contemplation easier in isolation from other human contacts. Such people often led the life of a recluse, perhaps in a hut high up in the mountains. Others could find revelation even in the humdrum, noisy atmosphere of city life. In fact, the philosophy may have been primarily intended for them, an attempt to help town-dwellers to avoid the mental strain of a high-speed, competitive existence.

Taoism taught that personal satisfaction could be attained by the individual. Confucianism maintained that it could result only from the greater achievement of complete social harmony. Only if people respected all classes of society would the security result in which a man could fully develop his capabilities. This humanistic philosophy was first suggested by Confucius, who stressed the values of sympathy, humility, sincerity, courtesy, and perseverance. It was taken up by Mencius, who made definite proposals for benevolent government based on the recorded sayings of Confucius.

Successive governments did indeed proclaim their adherence to Confucian principles, yet the Confucianism of practical administration was hardly that of earlier theory. It was more a complex system of ritual and law. Its object was certainly social harmony, out of consideration not so much for the rights of the individual envisaged by Mencius as for the protection and strengthening of the position of the officialdom. It emphasized subjection to authority and class distinctions.

Only in one respect were class barriers disregarded: State education was provided, and men with genuine talents could reach the highest posts in the government regardless of their background. The cynic might call this an astute move to deprive potential opposition of its leading brains. Whether or not this was the intention, the Confucian control over education helped the official class to exert authority over the whole of Chinese life throughout two thousand years, while imperial houses from the Han to the Ch'ing came and went; nor does the present state "religion," Communism, neglect this aspect of education.

Paper, Printing, and Book Production

Chinese officials were accustomed from a very early period to using books. Scribes of the Shang dynasty wrote on strips of bamboo or smooth slats of wood. These were strung together with hemp or silken cords and knotted between each "page." Writing on bamboo had to be done in vertical lines, and perhaps this is how the Chinese acquired the habit of writing in columns from the top to the bottom of a page. Nowadays, some books are still printed in the traditional style, reading from top to bottom, right to left, and starting at what we would call the back. Many are also produced in the Western style of horizontal lines, reading from left to right. A page of a newspaper may include articles set in both styles: The reader's eye must tell him where to begin.

Records and books were compiled on bundles of strips until the Han dynasty. Silk had been in use as a writing surface at least since the sixth century B.C., but it was more expensive than wood or bamboo and had the disadvantage of being heavy when rolled up in quantity. Although it continued to be chosen for special purposes until the T'ang dynasty, it never achieved the popularity of wood or, later, paper. After

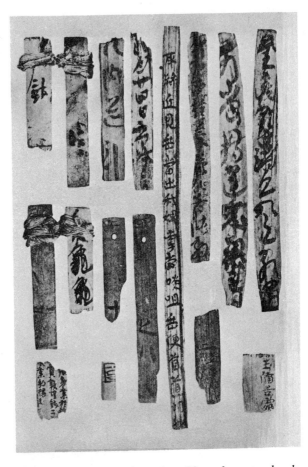

Plate 5. The remains of a Han dynasty book written on bamboo slips

the ninth century, silk was used principally for illustrations, maps, and paintings.

A citizen of the Han Empire, Ts'ai Lun, is credited with the invention of paper. He was Director of the Imperial Workshops, and, in A.D. 105, he presented this new type of writing surface at the court. It was more pliable than bamboo and not as bulky as silk. He made it by boiling together a collection of tree bark, rags, hemp, and fishing nets, straining the pulp, and allowing it to dry, spread out in the sun.

The earliest paper was very brittle, but techniques were quickly improved and a stronger kind of paper that could be rolled up was developed. The following formula for paper making from a seventeenth-century technical work shows that Ts'ai Lun's process had to be altered little in the course of time:

> Soak some strips of bamboo for one hundred days and then pound. Mix with liquid lime and boil for eight days and nights. Wash and strain the mixture with "the liquor of plant ashes." Repeat this process until the pulp is completely soft, then pound it again and bleach. Lay a number of "sheets" of the pulp on a draining frame and press them together. Dry the resulting sheet on a wall of firebricks, heated from behind. (*T'ien Kung K'ai Wu* (1637), ch. 13.)

Paper was not immediately accepted for all writing purposes. Even as late as the T'ang dynasty, the writer of an important document might apologize for using paper instead of silk, and this despite the variety of beautiful hand-made papers available to him in the shops. Here, in addition to the delicately colored Chinese papers, the discriminating purchaser might find imported papers from Japan or Southeast Asia, or perhaps the palmyra leaf from India.

The palmyra, or fan palm, leaf was sometimes used for copying religious texts because of its associations with India. In fact, it was the steady inflow of Buddhist teachers and translators and the increasing demand for their writings that gave the greatest boost to the production of paper and books. Books were now formed by pasting together the ends of a number of sheets of paper and attaching them to a roller. This in itself could produce a thing of beauty, the texture of the paper complementing the weight and feel of the fine wood and the decoration of the ivory knobs at each end. Furthermore, the scribe also had to be a calligrapher, and the attractiveness of his handwriting was an integral part of the whole.

Plate 6. The handwriting of the Sung Emperor Hui-tsung, a famous calligrapher

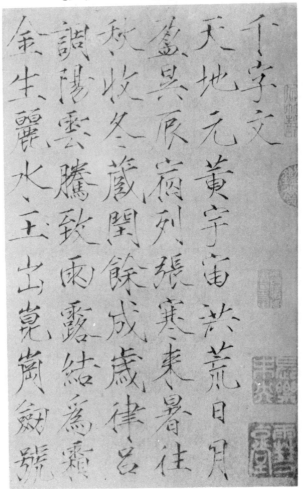

His tools were simple: They had changed little since the Shang dynasty and are still used today. His brush was a bamboo tube fitted with interchangeable tips of rabbit, deer or goat hairs. His ink was a solid stick, ground on a stone and mixed with water as required.

The formula used by a first-rate ink manufacturer was a closely guarded secret, but the essential ingredient was either lampblack or the soot from pine charcoal. Either of these had the property of giving the ink its jet-black color, and incidentally a permanence not characteristic of modern Western ink. A sixth-century agricultural encyclopedia, *Ch'i Min Yao Shu*, gives the following ingredients for one catty (about a pound) of ink. The recipe may have been used by the famous ink-maker Wei Tan (A.D. 179–253):

5 oz. pinewood soot, strained through silk
5 oz. best glue, dissolved in the juice of the bark of the *ch'in* tree
1 oz. cinnabar
1 oz. musk
5 egg whites

We may perhaps assume that Ennin was more interested in the Buddhist scriptures in the libraries than in the general works in the bookstalls. However, he must surely have browsed from time to time through the stocks of the Ch'ang-an shops. Their shelves carried books on a wide variety of subjects, reflecting the inquiring nature of the T'ang mind. There were copies of the standard Confucian, Taoist, and Buddhist texts. There were descriptive works on foreign lands and records of journeys overseas by clerical and lay travelers. There were foreign and Chinese medical books; books on mathematics, science, history, and astronomy; schoolbooks; and musical scores. Among the reference works were Chinese-Sanskrit and Chinese-Persian dictionaries.

Book-collectors and librarians were more likely to commission individual copies than to buy off the shelf. Private libraries were sometimes very large, running into tens of thousands of works. For storage purposes, scrolls were laid side by side on the shelves with their knobs to the outside. A general classification was made into four categories—classics, history, philosophy, and *belles lettres*—and the ivory knobs accordingly were painted red, blue, green, or white.

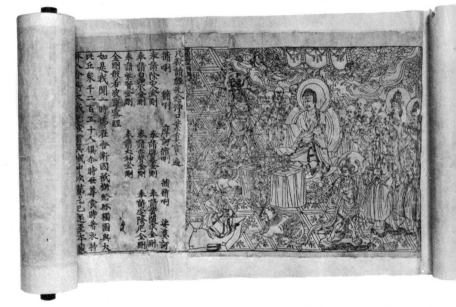

Plate 7. The world's oldest extant printed book, the Diamond Sutra, A.D. *868*

It is possible that Ennin saw books made in the latest ninth-century style. This consisted of a single length of stiff paper folded accordion-like, with a hard board at each end as a cover. The reader would pull open one fold at a time and read from the right. The new format was an important step in the progress from the scroll to the modern book, although it was still some 500 years before Chinese books took on the appearance that many modern publications retain. These are printed on thin sheets of rice paper and folded double. The pages are stitched together with silk or fine thread along the open side of the fold, and the whole is given a paper cover. A single book usually requires several volumes bound in this way. These are then presented in a stiff cloth cover, which folds around the paper sections and is fastened with two ivory tags.

It is also possible that Ennin saw examples of the most exciting invention of the T'ang dynasty, block printing. The earliest printed book still in existence dates from A.D. 868, at least one hundred years after the actual invention of the process. The printing of a book involved two men, the printer and a calligrapher. The printer prepared the wooden block, which was usually of pearwood, and covered it with a paste of boiled rice. The calligrapher wrote the text to be printed on a sheet of thin paper, which was then placed inverted on the block. After smoothing over the surface, the printer removed the paper and revealed an ink image of the original. He used a sharp tool to cut away all surface wood not covered by the ink, leaving the characters in fairly high relief. The block was then ready for inking.

Books were first printed in quantity by Feng Tao, who published the Confucian classics in 130 volumes between 932 and 953. One hundred years later, some time between 1041 and 1049, a man named Pi Sheng invented movable type. His main piece of equipment was a metal frame of vertical columns mounted on an iron plate. The inside surface of the plate was covered with wax. The pieces of type were made of baked clay, each inscribed with one character in reverse. Clay was used because it maintained its shape better when dampened by the ink: Wooden pieces were found to swell.

When setting up the font, the wax was melted and the pieces slipped into place under the frame. When the wax cooled, it gripped the type in place. Before inking, the printer smoothed over the surface of the plate with a board of pearwood to ensure that all pieces were perfectly level and that all characters would be applied evenly to the paper.

Printing techniques improved with time, but movable type has never entirely superseded block printing. The spirit of Chinese calligraphy cannot be contained on strictly regular pieces. Self-expression requires room for movement, the de-

Plate 8. A modern Chinese typewriter

The carriage (*A*) and the pickup mechanism move on rollers (*B*) over the tray of type. The operator places the pickup head (*C*) over the desired (reversed) character and depresses the lever (*D*). The piece is then mechanically lifted, inked on a felt roller (*E*), applied to the paper (*F*), and returned to its place, all in a split second.

velopment of individual style with conscious asymmetry. The artist gives the character life through the exaggeration of some of its strokes. At the same time, it remains perfectly balanced. To be able to achieve each of these qualities, movement and balance, is one mark of the good calligrapher. Since a printing block can be made to any dimensions, this method is ideal for the reproduction of calligraphy. To the Chinese, the preservation of fine handwriting is worth the extra trouble.

Further Reading

Ennin's diary is translated by Edwin O. Reischauer, *Ennin's Diary* (New York: Ronald, 1955), and elaborated in *Ennin's Travels in T'ang China* (New York: Ronald, 1955). An entertaining reconstruction of T'ang society is provided by the detective stories of R. van Gulik, e.g. *The Chinese Gold Murders* (London: Michael Joseph, 1959), *The Emperor's Pearl* (London: Heinemann, 1963). Factual but equally absorbing accounts are the books of Edward Schafer, *The Golden Peaches of Samarkand* (Berkeley, Cal.: University of California Press, 1963), and *The Vermilion Bird* (Berkeley, Cal.: University of California Press, 1967).

As an introduction to Chinese philosophy, see Wing-tsit Chan, *A Source Book in Chinese Philosophy* (Princeton, N.J.: Princeton University Press, 1963).

4

A Venetian in Yuan China

In 1279, the Mongols completed the final stage of their conquest of China. They had won the north from the usurping Chin dynasty, another non-Chinese people, forty-six years before. The legitimate Sung government, confined to southern China by the Chin since 1127, succumbed only after stiffer resistance. The Mongol chief was Kublai Khan, and when he became Emperor he was the first foreigner ever to rule over the whole of China. In fact, the area under his control extended even farther than that, from east China as far as Eastern Europe. It was one of the greatest empires in the history of the world.

Communications across the Asian continent were the best they had ever been. Perhaps that was how it came about that Marco Polo, a boy of seventeen, was allowed to accompany his father and uncle on their return visit to China. They sailed from Venice in 1271, left their ship at Acre on the coast of Syria, and then followed an overland route similar to that of the old Silk Road, traveling by way of Balk and Kashgar.

They arrived in China in May, 1275, and were received in Peking* at the magnificent court of the great Khan.

The Polos were taken into government service, and there began seventeen years of hard, fascinating work for Marco. The Emperor trusted him, and in time he was promoted to a high position, probably in the Salt and Iron Department. His work took him to all corners of the country. Wherever he went, he was amazed at the power of the ruler he served, the thoroughness of his military organization, and the sights and riches of the land. Ten years earlier, he had hardly heard of Cathay.* Now he was seeing for himself that it was as big as the whole of Europe and even more modern.

Space will not permit a description of life during the Sung and Yuan dynasties. Some idea of its advanced state will be suggested by the civilization of the Han and T'ang, on which it was built. It was progressive and exciting. So, for some, was life in contemporary Europe: It was the age of the early parliaments and the new universities; great cathedrals and castles were rising, expressing men's hopes and fears in incredible craftsmanship; and as for excitement, even the growing competition between merchant cities was no less dangerous than crusading, if less idealistic. In China, however, it was the details of life as well as the vast sweep of the panorama that impressed Marco Polo; things like paper money, public baths, paved streets with drainage, courier services, fire brigades, and the big ships built with watertight compartments.

Marco Polo left for home early in 1292, two years before Kublai Khan died. When he later dictated his account of China, some people dismissed it as over-fanciful. It certainly does contain exaggerations: For example, Hangchow did not have 12,000 bridges, as Marco says it did. It had 100 inside the city and 105 in the suburbs. We also know that as an official and a foreigner he kept aloof from the ordinary Chinese. He shows little sympathy for the life of the peasants, even when he notes: "Almost all the poor and needy sell some of their sons and daughters to the rich and noble, so that they may support themselves on the price paid for them, and the children may be better fed in their new homes." But these are natural failings, which do not detract from the importance of the book. It is the earliest description of China by a European eyewitness; it contains a fascinating account of the splendor of Peking and Kublai Khan's magnificent court; and the story is simply and entertainingly told.

Marco Polo's presence in China was not unique in any way. It was a long journey from Venice to China, though neither as daring nor as significant as those of Columbus or Vasco da Gama. He was not the first to make it: His father and uncle had reached the court of Peking in 1265. Their experience certainly made the second expedition less hazardous, since they carried as credentials a golden tablet, presented to them by the great Khan himself. Nor was Marco Polo the only European to live in China in the late thirteenth and early fourteenth centuries: Genoese merchants conducted enough trade there to warrant permanent warehouses. The papacy, too, established direct contact with Peking, and with the support of Kublai Khan and subsequent emperors the Catholic Church took root. In 1307 a Franciscan, John of Montecorvino, was created the first Archbishop of Cambaluc (Peking), and five years later he had five suffragan bishops with dioceses extending into southern China. The success of the missionary effort was short-lived. When the Mongol dynasty was swept away in 1368, the Christian Church went with it.

The historical merit of Marco Polo, finding expression in his book, derives from the variety of his interests. First, by coming from a merchant family, he naturally noticed and recorded the things people bought and sold, what they ate and what they paid for their purchases. Secondly, the object of the 1271 adventure was missionary as well as commercial.

It was the papacy's first response to Kublai Khan's request for one hundred Christian teachers. Two Dominican monks did in fact set out with the Polos but soon turned back. Marco himself was an active churchman and leaves a good commentary on the state of medieval Asian Christianity. Third, Marco had a good brain for administrative affairs, which is how he came to do well in the government and so describe its workings at first hand.

Chinese Nationalism

Having conquered China, the Mongols were in an awkward position with regard to ruling it. Their own political system, based on their way of life in the Central Asian steppes, had to do with a nomadic population having tribal leaders, cattle, camels, and horses. They did not know how to deal with an organization already working along different lines, with taxes assessed on permanent farmlands and crop yields, widespread irrigation schemes, and thousands of permanent civil servants.

Until the nineteenth century, peoples from the north and northwest were the only ones ever to invade China, and they all came from a similar, steppe background. Whenever a non-Chinese people established a dynasty, it faced this same problem. There were two solutions. The first was integration. This meant an attempt on the part of the conquerors to learn and adopt Chinese ways and to accept Chinese help in matters of government. It was not a theory of racial equality, for the rulers insisted on privileges for their own people. However, under dynasties adopting this principle, such as the (Northern) Wei (386–535), the Chinese had more and more say in their own affairs and usually succeeded in completely sinicizing* their governors.

The alternative to integration was domination by the conquering minority. This was attempted by the Yuan (Mongols) and the Ch'ing (Manchus, 1644–1911). The Ch'ing quickly found the policy unworkable and resorted to a scheme of qualified integration. Government posts were duplicated by Manchus and Chinese, each looking after their own peoples' interests. In some activities, such as farming, the Chinese had to help the Manchus with jobs to which they were unaccustomed. Having made these concessions, the Manchus would not give any more. They emphasized their position as conquerors in many ways. For example, they devised easier tests for Manchu candidates in the civil service examinations. They also ordered all Chinese to wear their hair in a pigtail. This law was naturally unpopular, and the custom died out after the end of the dynasty in 1911. Until quite recently, however, it was still occasionally possible to see an elderly gentleman in Hong Kong wearing his hair in this style.

The Manchu policy of rule was the reverse of the Mongol. Kublai Khan had begun with attempts at conciliation: The government patronized the arts and public charities, it built hospitals and old peoples' homes, it proclaimed freedom of religious practices, all in an attempt to win the support of the top Chinese intellectuals. The Chinese, however, would not cooperate. They had been contented under the Sung and had fought stubbornly for them. While they now submitted passively to their new rulers, only a few would help them. Sometimes Kublai Khan tried to force them to. In 1289, a man named Hsieh Fang-te starved to death rather than give assistance under compulsion. Kublai Khan soon realized that he could not rely on Chinese support.

The Mongols then embarked on a policy of severe racial discrimination. They brought specialists in government from all over Asia so that they would not need Chinese assistance. Marco Polo, whose arrival in Peking was coincidental, was probably the only European to be offered a post. A college was opened where Mongols could learn Chinese, but most of the new officials understood neither the Chinese people nor their language. Yet they were supposed to work among them, collect their taxes, fill in their census forms, check their movements, and generally enforce the law. The Chinese found them easy prey for trickery.

Two sets of laws were introduced, one for Mongols and one, harsher, for Chinese. No intermarriage was allowed. Private lands were confiscated from the Chinese. Restrictions were placed on their housing, clothing, and carriages, and a curfew was imposed. They were not allowed to own weapons or horses; they could not learn to fence or hunt, nor to speak the Mongol language. The upper classes found the best jobs closed to them, and in everything there was a bias in favor of the Mongols.

There was no quick rising against the numerically weaker Mongols. For one thing, their cavalry forces were large and efficient. For another, those Chinese families that had been rich in Sung times still lived comfortably enough to discourage them from active protest, and the poor were too intent on their vital work in the fields. When the dynasty was finally overthrown, it was not because of its racial policy but because of increasingly bad administration.

The striking thing about all periods of foreign rule in China is that there was never any general opposition on the grounds of race. Of course all such dynasties fell in time, but the rebels who overthrew them never fought against "foreigners" so much as against "corrupt officials." As long as the machinery of government functioned well, no matter who controlled it, the Chinese would not interfere with it. This was part of Confucian teaching in action. Furthermore, the Chinese knew that they were the greatest people on earth. This was self-evident, they said, from their superior culture and way of life. They attracted the attention of other states. Consequently, they were not seriously perturbed when, from time to time, non-Chinese rulers came to power. They believed that the conquerors would eventually succumb to Chinese civilization, and then things would go on just as before. They were usually right. Even the Mongols were less particularistic in the end.

In the nineteenth century, China came up against the full power of the West, military, religious, diplomatic, and commercial. For the first time, confidence in Chinese invincibility was shaken. Europe would not submit to Chinese ideas. After much soul-searching, it was the Chinese who gave way, and the modernization of government and industry began.

China now had to stand up for itself. It had to fight for its rights, for it could no longer command automatic respect from other countries. As an initial step, a new surge of patriotism was needed. The spectacle of Europe at war between 1914 and 1918 helped to produce this, and it was fostered by government propaganda, teaching in schools, lectures, and newspaper and magazine articles. During the 1920's, a wave of anti-foreign and anti-Christian feeling led to strikes, violence, and severe restrictions on foreign schools: the people were doing their part. But even the Nationalist Party, first under Sun Yat-sen and then under Chiang Kai-shek, was unable to follow their lead and emphasize China's position in international affairs. World War II intervened, China was occupied by the Japanese, and patriotism seemed doomed.

Since 1949, the Communist regime has successfully revived it. Every possible medium of mass persuasion—radio, television, films, newspapers, wall posters, and public meetings—presents the Chinese case on major issues, such as the Vietnam war. Anti-foreign propaganda pours out in such well-known clichés as "U.S. Imperialists" and "U.S. Aggressors." The emphasis is generally on the hostile intentions of America and Russia toward China. Its leaders may or may not believe in these themselves, but they are good psychologists. They know that a people wound up almost to fever pitch for a war effort will tighten its belt more willingly and work harder. There may be more than 800 million Chinese. Their sense of nationalism is unparalleled throughout the world. They wholeheartedly support their government's modernizing ambitions. Yet their determination to restore China's greatness must be distinguished, as it could be in the past, from narrow racialism. A Chinese retains a peculiar pride in his race wherever in the world he happens to be born or wherever political events drive him. However, it is nationalism, not racialism, that drives China today. Before the Cultural Revolution*, it was China's boast that the 50 million non-Chinese, the national minority peoples who lived within its borders, shared its ambitions. These included Koreans, Tibetans, Mongols, and many other racial groups. The aim was that all should eventually constitute self-governing states within a Chinese "Commonwealth" system. Until then, their own way of life and interests were protected and catered to by the government, in which they were represented. They were an integrated part of the whole union. It is known, however, that the Cultural Revolution created disenchantment among some of the racial minorities, and not enough is yet known about their present state of allegiance nor of the attitude of the government toward them.

Chinese Inventions and Discoveries

There have been many links between East and West. Some are mentioned in this book, and more detailed accounts will be found elsewhere. One aspect of these relations can be studied in the series of books by Dr. Joseph Needham entitled *Science and Civilization in China.*[1] Here, with the aid of illustrations, diagrams, and quotations from original sources, Dr.

[1] Cambridge, England: Cambridge University Press, 1954–. In seven volumes, of which four have so far appeared.

Needham describes the inventions and discoveries of the Chinese and compares them with counterpart scientific knowledge in other parts of the world. This fascinating project is not yet complete, but three points already emerge from it.[2]

(1) *Before the European Renaissance, the Chinese were the superiors of the West in many fields of knowledge.* Their mechanical skill led to the invention of such precision instruments as the Han dynasty's crossbow trigger (Fig. 4) and the

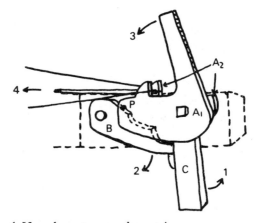

Figure 4. A Han dynasty crossbow trigger

Numbers indicate the sequence of movements as the trigger (*C*) is pulled. *P* is a pin connecting plates A_1 and A_2 and resting on top of plate *B* until allowed to drop. As A_1/A_2 falls forward, the string is released and the bolt propelled.

water-driven mechanical clocks of the eighth to the thirteenth century (Fig. 5). These were more accurate than the first European clocks of the fourteenth century, though after the invention of the pendulum the performance of European clocks soon surpassed that of the Chinese.

[2] These are not, of course, the only conclusions to be drawn from Dr. Needham's work, nor is it his sole intention to prove these points.

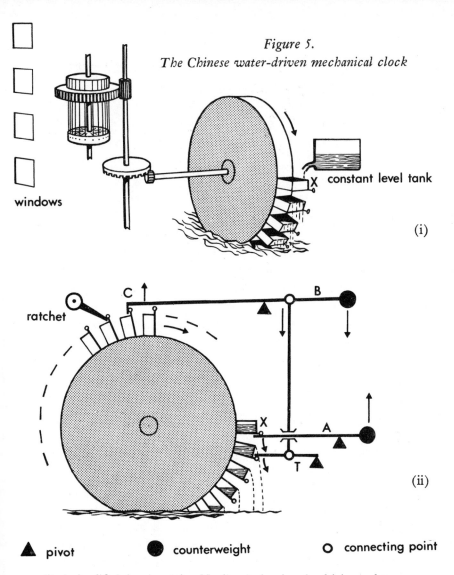

Figure 5.
The Chinese water-driven mechanical clock

windows

constant level tank

(i)

ratchet

C

B

X

A

T

(ii)

▲ pivot   ● counterweight   ○ connecting point

(i) A simplified drawing (after Needham) showing the driving and transmission shafts of the water clock. Figures were mounted on a number of horizontal wheels and could be viewed through five windows in the clock tower as they rotated. Their relative positions indicated the time of day.

(ii) A diagram (after Needham) showing the escapement system which controlled the movement of the driving wheel. When the bucket at position X was filled with water, it tipped the balance arm (A) and fell onto the trip lever (T). As this in turn fell, it pulled down the balance arm (B) and momentarily lifted the catch (C), allowing the buckets to move forward one place. Water overflowing from the buckets then allowed the balance (A) to rock the wheel back against the ratchet, and the process was gradually repeated.

*Plate 9. The trigger mechanism of a Han
dynasty crossbow, top view. Length,
4 inches; width, 1½ inches; depth, 1½
inches.*

Their scientists made discoveries and learned to apply them.
Iron was being cast in the third century B.C., steel manufac-
tured by a very advanced process in the sixth century A.D.,
and fine porcelain made in the eleventh century. The Sung
dynasty in particular was a period of extraordinary progress.
Pride of place among its inventions must surely go to the
magnetic compass and the development of gunpowder. Gunpowder had first been mixed during the eighth century but
was not brought under control for use in warfare until the
Sung. The barrel gun, ancestor of all modern cannon, was
first used against the Chin invaders early in the twelfth
century.

Even before the T'ang dynasty, Chinese doctors kept
comprehensive stocks of herbs and medicines, and when in
doubt there were medical books to which they could refer.

Cures were not effected by oral means alone. Anatomy was studied and an ancient form of treatment called acupuncture used. According to the patient's symptoms, the doctor would insert thin needles into his body at specific points (Plate 10). This was believed to resolve internal tensions, restore natural bodily harmony, and cure the patient. European doctors used to regard this idea as superstitious nonsense, but it is now widely believed, in the West as well as in China, that acupuncture has a therapeutic effect. The stimulation of the needles seems to affect the sympathetic nervous system and to stiffen the patient's resistance to disease. Specialists in the West offer

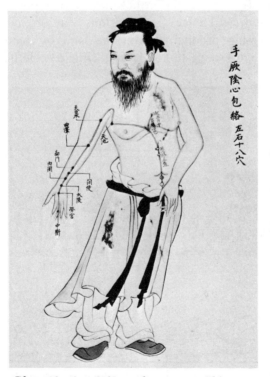

Plate 10. An eighteenth-century Chinese acupuncture chart

this kind of treatment for a wide variety of complaints, including malaria, tuberculosis, rheumatism, bronchitis, appendicitis, migraine, and insomnia. Sufferers from all sorts of illnesses confirm that it gives them relief.

(2) *The Chinese thought a great deal about labor-saving devices.* This is not to say that they lacked pure scientists or pure mathematicians, but only that the need to grow food was always more pressing than the need for knowledge for its own sake. As the population increased, so did its demand for food. As the wealth of the country increased, so did the number of nonfarmers in proportion to that of farmers. It was essential to make the utmost use of manpower and of natural resources. Hence, (i) inventions were often concerned with increasing productivity on the land by reducing the amount of work done by the farmer (Fig. 6). He might then

Figure 6. A multiple trip-hammer for pounding grain, from T'ien Kung K'ai Wu (1637)

do two jobs in the time formerly taken by one. (ii) Labor-saving devices for industry would release more workers for the "basic industry" (agriculture). Figure 7 shows a blowing engine, which probably originated in the iron and steel industry foundries of the tenth century. As the rotary motion of the water wheel was converted into longitudinal motion by the use of crank *(a)*, swinging link *(b)*, and connecting rod *(c)*, the furnace bellows were opened and shut and a continuous draft was produced. The furnace could then be kept at a high temperature indefinitely. The invention used a plentiful and free source of power, running water. The water wheel had been in use since the early Han dynasty, lifting water for irrigation and driving grain pounders and grinders. Later its applications were more ingenious, as in Figures 5 and 7. By the fourteenth century, the textile industry had also learned to harness water power for use in spinning mills.

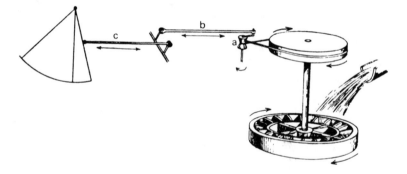

Figure 7. A simplified diagram of a blowing engine (after Needham)

(3) *Many Chinese discoveries and inventions were copied in the West and their origins forgotten.* It is well known that the West acquired its liking for tea, rice, and silk from China, but not so often realized that the same country first sent us

rhubarb, lacquer, and honeysuckle also. The list of "imports" from the East is really very long. It includes items of major significance in Western history, such as paper, printing, gunpowder, and the compass. It includes more than a few everyday objects: the banknote, wallpaper (as opposed to tapestry), the wheelbarrow, the kite, the stirrup, and the examination paper. Even our outlook on society and government has been influenced indirectly by the Chinese, for Voltaire, Rousseau, and other eighteenth-century European philosophers were admirers of Confucian ideas.

It is not difficult to see how knowledge was transmitted from East to West. Sometimes the story, the sketch, even perhaps the article in question itself was carried across Asia by merchants or soldiers, to be picked up by Europeans in the Middle East. Sometimes communication was direct, and the Europeans returned from Asia with firsthand experience: There were those who visited Mongol China; the Portuguese traders of the sixteenth century, followed in the seventeenth by members of the East India Companies; and the Jesuit priests of the seventeenth and eighteenth centuries.

Surely the Polo family itself brought back ideas, though Marco only hints at China's technical progress in his book. He was impressed with their skill in bridge-building. This is a branch of architecture in which the Chinese have always combined utility with aesthetics. Here is his description of the bridges at Chengtu, in Szechwan province:

The branch streams within the city are crossed by stone bridges of great size and beauty. They are eight paces in width, and in length up to half a mile according to the width of the stream. Along the bridges on either side are fine columns of marble that support the roof: For all the bridges are covered with handsome wooden roofs richly decorated and painted in red. The roofing is of tiles. All along the bridges on either side are rows of booths devoted to the practice of various forms of trade and craft. They are wooden structures, erected every morning and taken down at night.

Certain types of bridge in China were new to Marco Polo. One was the wide, arched bridge with a single span. Most Chinese arches were semicircular (Fig. 8 [*i*]), and when the river to be crossed was wide it was usual to join more than one arch together (Fig. 8 [*ii*]). By the seventh century, how-

Figure 8. The traditional Chinese bridge

ever, the Chinese had learned to do without the central piers by shaping and fitting the stone segments into a single flying "flat" arc. This is known as the segmental arch bridge. Li Ch'un built a beautiful one at Chaohsien, in Hopei, in A.D. 610, which is still standing (Fig. 9). Its stones are fastened to-

Figure 9. The An-chi bridge at Chao-hsien, Hopei

gether with iron clamps for additional strength. The understanding of structural dynamics involved in building such a bridge was greatly advanced. The first European segmental arch bridge did not appear until 1345, in Florence.

In 1278, Marco Polo was sent by Kublai Khan on a mission
to what is now part of Burma. On his way through southwest
China he probably crossed the river gorges by suspension
bridge. In his time, many of these were borne on iron chains.
Before the Sui dynasty, ropes of twisted bamboo were used
instead. Figure 10 shows a bridge at Kuanhsien, in Szechwan.

Figure 10. The suspension bridge at Kuan-hsien, Szechwan

It was built in the second century B.C. by a famous governor
of Shu and hydraulic engineer, Li Ping, and is still maintained
according to his original specifications. For more than 2,000
years, the bamboo ropes have been regularly inspected and
replaced where necessary. The result is a perfect modern
example of ancient civil engineering.

It is strange that Marco Polo does not mention the suspension bridges, for they were not seen in Europe until 1741. But
there are many surprising omissions from his tale. He describes
the Grand Canal,* which Kublai Khan extended to connect
Peking and Hangchow. He is amazed at the "very large ships"
using the canal, yet he does not reveal that the Chinese were
building big paddleboats, undreamed of in Venice. He describes battles and sieges and yet gives no suggestion of the
use of gunpowder. Even if he did not see it for himself, he
must have heard stories of the strange weapons of the Sung
defenders. Perhaps the explanation for his silence is the same
as that given by Friar Odoric, ending his own description of
China in 1330: "Many strange things also I have of purpose

omitted, because men will not believe them unless they see them."

Further Reading

Many books have been written about Marco Polo. His own description of his travels is translated by R. E. Latham, *The Travels of Marco Polo* (Baltimore: Penguin, 1958). An interesting secondhand account, superbly illustrated, is that of M. Rugoff and L. Goodrich, *Marco Polo's Adventures in China* (New York: Harper and Row, 1964). This is a book that should be in every school library.

Two books that consider the contacts between Europe and China are Luce Boulnois, *The Silk Road* (New York: Dutton, 1966), and G. F. Hudson, *Europe and China* (Boston: Beacon Press, 1961).

Only a few of the many notable Chinese inventions have been mentioned in this book. Dr. Needham summarizes the effects of the greatest in *The Legacy of China*, ed. Raymond Dawson (New York: Oxford University Press, 1964). This book contains useful essays on various aspects of Chinese civilization and their contribution to world culture.

5

An Italian in Ming China

To celebrate the New Year 1588, Lord Burghley presented Queen Elizabeth I with "one porringer of white purselyn garnished with gold," and to Robert Cecil he gave "a cup of greene pursselyne." This was Chinese porcelain, much admired in sixteenth-century Europe. Only a few pieces reached England, though late in that century and early in the next Chinese export arrangements became more organized and supplies improved. Then, however, the quality was not so high, for the Chinese kept the best for their own use.

The porcelain was brought to Europe by Spanish or Portuguese ships and had probably been taken from China by pirates. They were a frequent source of trouble around the coasts of Ming China, as they had been under the previous dynasty, the Yuan. The worst offenders in the sixteenth century were the Japanese and the Portuguese. However, after the latter had been given permission in 1557 to settle on a peninsula, called Macao,* on the south China coast, they acquired more respectability and began to seek regular trading relations. Before the end of the dynasty in 1644, sea trade was booming. Tea, silk, and porcelain were exchanged for wine, glass, wool, precious stones, and watches. The ports of Macao, Canton, and Ningpo thrived on it. The Spaniards watched enviously from their nearby colony in the Philippines but were unable to take part, for Portugal had the backing of the papacy in claiming China as its particular sphere of influence.

Wherever the merchant of Renaissance Europe went, the Church was not far behind. The King of Portugal invited the Society of Jesus, the Jesuits, to send missionaries to the East. Their first successes beyond India were in Japan, reached by Francis Xavier in 1549, but attention soon turned to China. In 1576, Macao was made a diocese under the patronage of the King of Portugal.

In August, 1582, the Italian Father Matteo Ricci arrived in Macao. He was the ninth Jesuit priest to go there. He was only thirty, yet he was already one of the outstanding scientists and mathematicians in Europe. He had some training in classics and law, as well as a knowledge of astronomy and cosmology; he found foreign languages no difficulty. In short, his intellectual capabilities were enormous.

In the summer of 1583, Father Michele Ruggieri, another Italian, who had been in Macao since 1579, was sent to Canton. Matteo Ricci accompanied him to gain his first experience of China. It was the Jesuits' third attempt within a few months to gain a foothold in China proper, but the Japanese and Portuguese raids had aroused considerable prejudice against the presence of foreigners in the coastal provinces. Perhaps there were also memories of the chauvinism that had accompanied the overthrow of the Mongols and the return of a Chinese dynasty. The Viceroy of Kwangtung sent them back, disappointed, to Macao.

Then, within a week, a message arrived from Chao-ch'ing, an important town sixty miles west of Canton. It invited them to

build a house and church there on land that the local authorities would provide. It seemed too good to be true. Yet by
the middle of September, there they were, meeting the governor, choosing a site, provided with free travel permits, and
planning how to make contact with the crowds of people who
came to look at them. Says Ricci: "Rumors had spread about,

Plate 11. Matteo Ricci

with the customary exaggeration of this country, about
strangers with peculiar faces and other European peculiarities,
never before seen in China."

If the Chinese were intrigued with the foreigners, the Europeans were no less interested in their new neighbors. Ricci,
like Ennin before him, wrote down his observations, though
in far greater detail than the Japanese monk. Something new
to him was the habit of tea-drinking:

There is a certain bush from the leaves of which is decocted that celebrated drink, known to the Chinese, the Japanese, and their neighbors as Cia. . . . It might be that this same plant can be found in our own fields. . . . The Japanese brew their drink from these leaves in a slightly different way from the Chinese. They reduce them to powder and then place two or three teaspoonfuls of the powder in a pot of boiling water and drink the resulting beverage. The Chinese place some of the dried leaves in a pot of boiling water and when the water has extracted the virtue from the leaves, they strain off the leaves and drink what is left.

The Chinese today still make tea in this way.

The site chosen for the church was in the corner of a pleasant field next to a river. A pagoda was being built in the same field. The Jesuits quickly settled into their home for the next six years. Their immediate task was to dispel any doubts the local officials might have had about the safety of allowing them to stay.

Their approach to this problem was the right one: They tried to understand and abide by Chinese laws and etiquette; they began to learn the language and study the Chinese classics; and they appealed directly to the intellectual snobbery of the educated class. Ricci was not one to neglect the interests of working-class people, with whom he was happy to mix, but he recognized the importance of earning the respect of the men in power. In China, respect was paid more to evidence of scholarship than to shows of sympathy for the peasantry.

So tactful were the Jesuits that the mission house became a center of attraction for scholars in the province. They appreciated the appearance of the well-bound books in the library and were curious about the Catholic statues and pictures. The fathers presented Christianity as an ethical system compatible with Confucianism. By comparing it with something the Chinese already knew, they had a better chance of making their beliefs understood.

The Chinese visitors were particularly interested in the clocks and prisms and astronomical instruments in the mission and spent long hours listening to Ricci on the subject of European science. The map of the world hanging on the wall also provoked discussion. The Chinese themselves had produced, in the eleventh century, the earliest relief maps in the world, and only some thirty years before, in 1555, there had appeared an enlarged world atlas printed in grid, mostly concerned with China of course, but showing a good idea of the shape of Africa.

Although the Jesuits made many friends in high places, things were not always easy for them. Friendship with officials was unlikely to ensure popularity at large. Sometimes the mission house was stoned, and once the fathers had to face a trumped-up court charge. In 1589, a new Viceroy ordered them out of Chao-ch'ing. Fortunately they were offered new accommodation at Shao-chou, farther to the north, and the work began again. In 1594, Ricci took to wearing the dress of a Confucian scholar.

Matteo Ricci's ambition was to reach Peking, and in May, 1595, the chance seemed to have come. An eminent official had a son of twenty who was badly depressed at failing an examination. The official was being recalled to the capital, and he invited Ricci to join his entourage to look after his son. The journey began well enough, but between Kanchow and Chi-an, first the boat of the women and children was wrecked, and then Ricci's own vessel overturned. He was a poor swimmer and was lucky not to drown. The official decided to continue his journey overland. He wanted to send Ricci back to Shao-chou but was finally persuaded to let him carry on as far as Nanking.

Nanking was the second city of the Ming Empire and in

its most densely populated area. Ricci commented on the city's "gaiety of spirit." *Ming* means "bright," and Ricci had already been struck by the Chinese love of color. It was splashed everywhere, on the buildings, in the flower gardens, on the sedan chairs and decorative fans, on the porcelain, in the lavish fireworks displays. At one of these, Ricci calculated that "they consumed enough powder to carry on a sizable war for a number of years."

He was not allowed to stay long in Nanking and returned to the capital of Kiangsi, Nanchang, where he met with better fortune. He was able to buy a small house for sixty gold pieces, and it was while he was in Nanchang, in 1596, that he was made Superior of the whole China Mission.

Ricci's ambition was realized in 1598. Late in June, a former acquaintance who was now no less than President of the *Li Pu** visited him in Nanchang and invited him to go with him to Peking. They were accompanied by Father Cattaneo, another Italian, and two Chinese postulants. First they went to Nanking, which was in the grip of spy fever following a Japanese invasion of Korea, and then northward up the Grand Canal. The Europeans were fascinated by all they saw. Ricci wrote:

So great is the number of boats that frequently many days are lost in transit by crowding each other, particularly when water is low in the canals. To prevent this, the water is held back at stated places by wooden locks, which also serve as bridges. . . . At times it happens that the rush of water is so high and strong, at the exit from one lock or at the entrance to another, that the boats are capsized and the whole crew is drowned. The boats of the Magistrates and of other Government dignitaries are drawn up the stream, against the current, by wooden devices on the shore, and the expense for such hauling is paid by the Government. . . . The boats called cavaliers are commanded by palace eunuchs, and they always travel rapidly, in fleets of

eight or ten. The canal is navigable only in the summer season,
when the water is high, perhaps due to the melting of the snow
on the mountains where the river takes its rise. During the
hot summer season much of the foodstuffs, which are perhaps
a month or two in transportation, would spoil before reaching
Peking; so they are kept in ice to preserve them. The ice
gradually melts, and so great stores of it are kept at certain
stops, and the boats are liberally supplied with enough of it to
keep their cargoes fresh until arrival. The eunuchs sometimes
let out the vacant cabins on their palace boats for hire, and
keep the money. [At Tientsin] the whole river was covered
with ships of war, laden with troops, but the cavalier in which
the Fathers were traveling wedged its way between their
prows without interruption.

During the Ming dynasty the population drifted to the
north, reversing the trend of the Southern Sung and Yuan
periods. Peking was now an overcrowded city, not yet
adapted to its new requirements. The streets were mostly un-
paved, dirty, and inadequate for both pedestrians and the
great traffic of horses and sedan chairs. The houses were dull
and the narrow alleys shut off at night by iron grills. The
Inner City was more attractive.

The President of the *Li Pu* and a palace eunuch came to see
the presents the Jesuits had brought for the Emperor.

Father Matthew showed them the clock, the crucifix, a statue
of the Virgin Mother, a clavichord, the like of which the
Chinese had never heard of, and two triangular glass prisms.
When the statue of the Blessed Virgin was being lifted down
to the floor, it fell out of the hands of the carriers and was
broken into three pieces. That would have ruined its value in
Europe, but served only to increase it in China. When the
pieces were put together again, the statue took on an appearance of antiquity; which made it more valuable than when
it was whole.

The Chinese distrust of foreigners and their own dwindling reserves of money forced the visitors to leave Peking at the approach of winter. Ricci went on ahead and arrived in Soochow in style:

> They use a cart, built over a single wheel, on which one person sits astride in the center, as he would on a horse, with two others sitting, one on either side. This cart or wagon is pushed by a driver by means of wooden shafts. It affords a safe and a speedy means of travel, and it was thus that Father Matthew arrived in Suceu.

Soochow was a beautiful and prosperous port, and Ricci hoped to open a new house there. In February, 1599, he returned to Nanking to seek the permission he required. This time, however, the officials would have him stay in Nanking. A house was found for sale at a reasonable price—it was supposed to be haunted—and once again Ricci began the round of banquets and meetings with leading citizens.

A frequent topic of conversation was astronomy, for Nanking had a fine observatory. In the seventeenth century it became one of the missionaries' main interests to "teach" the Chinese about science and astronomy. In some respects the Chinese benefited from this: They learned, for example, to make instruments, to use the telescope, and to apply the principles of geometry in astronomy and surveying. In other ways they were the losers, as when the Jesuit Fathers "corrected" their conception of the stars as floating bodies in infinite empty space with their own idea of solid spheres and ten skies.

In one branch of science, meteorology, the Europeans could well have learned from the Chinese. Centuries of dependence on the weather had led them to take a special interest in natural phenomena. They had rain and snow gauges and kept daily weather records; they used kites to test wind behavior; they recorded rainbows, sun halos, and eclipses. Contrary to his own belief, Matteo Ricci was not the first to explain to the Chinese the reason for eclipses: Their own famous Royal Astronomer Chang Heng (A.D. 78–139) had done it in the first century A.D., nor was he the first.

Chang Heng was the inventor of the world's first seismograph. China lies in the earthquake belt—Nanking alone suffered 110 during the Ming dynasty—and the means of recording the occurence and approximate direction of an earthquake long before messengers could reach the capital was of enormous benefit to the authorities in organizing assistance. Relief works were provided not because the government sympathized with the stricken peasantry but because the rich families were anxious about their own food supplies. Chang Heng's invention was an ingenious mechanism: Around a domed vessel sat eight bronze toads with their mouths open. Above them were eight dragons' heads, each with a ball in its mouth. When an earth tremor occurred, the ball fell from the mouth of one of the dragons into the waiting mouth of the toad. The direction of the disturbance could be deduced by observing which of the dragons had dropped its ball. The *Hou Han Shu* says that the success of the seismograph was uncanny.

The span of the Ming dynasty was nearly exhausted, and in Peking and Nanking Ricci saw signs of decay. Petty crime, drunkenness, and pornographic literature were widespread. Upper-class morals were little better than those of the lower classes. The Emperor Wan-li was a despot who ruled only for his own pleasure. Of the nobility, Ricci wrote: "They have developed into a leisure class given to loose living and to insolence." The administration was in the hands of eunuchs who were hopelessly corrupt.

The eunuchs, as a class, are unlettered and barbarous, lacking shame and piety, utterly arrogant and very monsters of vice. What with these semi-men in command, and their greed developing them into savages, the whole kingdom was . . . in a worse state than it was during the Korean war. The war was external. This evil was from within, and greater, because of the fear it developed. Pilfering, cheating and robbery were everywhere common. The tax and customs bureaus were veritable dens of thieves.

Ricci was witnessing a social upheaval. Taxation in kind had been replaced by a monetary levy. People who previously had never used money now needed some. To raise it, they had to buy and sell. They neglected the land and drifted into the towns. Prices rose, but so did consumer demands. Industries were kept working at full capacity, especially those that also had to supply the export market. Southern Kiangsu and northern Chekiang were the boom areas, and Soochow was the center of the greatest urban development. The rich grew richer and the poor poorer.

The upheaval produced no fundamental change in the traditional structure of society. Agriculture remained the basic industry, and Confucian officials continued to run the country, even after the Manchu conquest. It did, however, have certain side effects, among which were the development of the novel and the growth of the theater: People in the new towns needed entertainment. Ricci wrote:

I believe this people is too much interested in dramatic representations and shows. At least they certainly surpass us in this respect. An exceedingly large number of the youth of the land is devoted to this activity. Some of them form traveling troupes which journey everywhere throughout the length and breadth of the country, while other groups reside permanently in the large centers and are in great demand for private as well as for public performances.

Matteo Ricci returned to Peking, this time for good, in 1601. The presents and the intellectual abilities of the Jesuits so attracted the attention of the Emperor that he not only granted their petition to stay in the capital but actually ar-

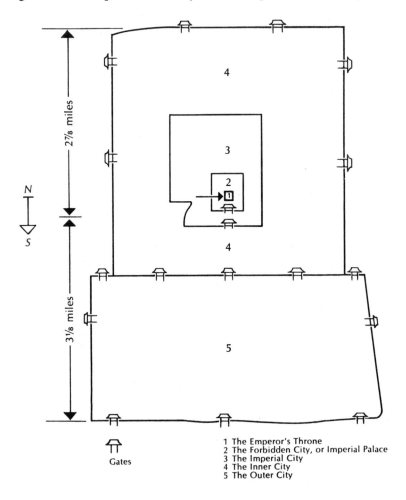

2⅞ miles

3⅛ miles

N

S

Gates

1 The Emperor's Throne
2 The Forbidden City, or Imperial Palace
3 The Imperial City
4 The Inner City
5 The Outer City

Map 5. Peking in the early seventeenth century

ranged for them to receive an official grant every four months. Throughout the remaining nine years of his life, Ricci labored unceasingly, teaching, debating, writing, and translating. He earned so high a reputation that following his death in May, 1610, the court granted a house and grounds tax-free to his Order, and it was here that he was laid to rest.

Ricci was perhaps the greatest of all Jesuit missionaries. There were no more than 2,500 Christians in the Chinese Empire when he died, a tiny fraction of the total population of more than 50 million. His achievement was to have laid such secure foundations that for more than 150 years both European and Chinese Christians were able to hold positions of much influence and authority in the Government of China. Outstanding in this respect were the Jesuit Fathers Schall, a German, and Verbiest, a Belgian. Both of these men were confidential advisers to Emperors in an age in which few ministers even saw the monarch.

But China was not to be converted. The growth of the Christian community in the seventeenth century withered away in the eighteenth. There were several reasons for this: (1) The Manchus, being foreigners, needed to gain Chinese support. Therefore they embraced Confucianism at the ultimate expense of Christianity. (2) The danger from underground political sects increased and the foreign religion was regarded with more suspicion. (3) As European missionary zeal declined, so did manpower and funds for the China field. (4) The Church itself blackened its own image for all time in the eyes of the Chinese by revealing its own divisions, first through the differences between the eighteenth-century missionary Orders, the Jesuits, Franciscans, Dominicans, and so on, and second through the dispute that split the Jesuit Order itself, over whether to permit or to forbid Christian participation in any Chinese customs or ceremonies that might contain so-called pagan elements. These include civil ceremonies in which the name of Confucius was used and many private customs in which family ancestors were honored. Matteo Ricci had set a precedent for making concessions to traditional Chinese beliefs, but after bitter wrangling the Church finally forbade it.

Until the Cultural Revolution there was still a Catholic Church in China. It was officially tolerated and could practice without interference provided that it accepted the supremacy of the civil authorities over its temporal affairs and taught nothing contrary to the interests of the state. These were the conditions Ricci accepted and the papacy rejected. They were accepted by Chinese Catholics after 1949 but were again rejected by the papacy. The Chinese Catholic Church no longer remained in communion with the Church of Rome. Christian churches and Buddhist temples were closed in 1966, and the fate of those known to be regular worshippers at them has not been revealed.

CHRONOLOGICAL CHART: CHRISTIANITY IN CHINA

1514	The Portuguese reach China.
	Papal Bull permits Portuguese to exclude missionaries of their rivals.
1580	Jesuit missionary training center established at Macao. Union of the crowns of Spain and Portugal (until 1640).
1585	Papal brief forbids any attempts to enter China other than *(a)* by Jesuits and *(b)* via Lisbon and Goa, i.e., no Dominicans or Franciscans from the Philippines. They had attempted to settle in 1575, 1579, 1582, and 1585, and continued to do so. Both orders had provinces that included the Philippines and China.
1600	The Pope removes first part of the 1585 restriction. Founding of the British East India Company.

1608	The Pope removes second part of the 1585 restriction.
1611	de Ursis (Jesuit astronomer) entrusted with the reform of the Chinese Imperial Calendar and the translation of European books on astronomy.
1616	First persecution of Christianity in China. Jesuits lose control of the Board of Astronomy until 1629.
1625 *c.*	The Spanish establish a post on Formosa. Dominicans and Franciscans use it to enter Fukien.
1632	Fr. Schall celebrates Mass for the first time in the Imperial Palace. Influential in having Christianity accepted at court was Ricci's most famous convert, Paul Hsü (Hsü Kuang-ch'i), now made a Grand Secretary.
1637	Dominicans and Franciscans driven out of Fukien.
1640	Beginning of the concessions, or "rites," controversy.
1642	The Dutch drive the Spanish out of Formosa.
1643–1715	Louis XIV King of France.
1644	Manchu conquest of China. Emperor Shun-shih (1644–61; with regent 1644–51). Schall retained as a director of the Board of Astronomy, where he gains great influence over the Emperor.
1645	Papal decree forbidding concessions in the official Roman Catholic attitude toward traditional Chinese beliefs, many of which were considered pagan.
1656	Papal decree permitting such concessions.
1662–1722	Emperor K'ang-hsi; was strongly influenced by the head of the Jesuit mission, Fr. Verbiest. His great reign was a period of encouragement for Christians in China.
	Over the next hundred years, at least 216 foreign embassies were received in Peking.
1673	Secular clergy permitted to go to China.
1687	The first French Jesuits reach China, sent by Louis XIV. They include Lecomte.
1690	Two new sees created, Peking and Nanking; patronage given to the King of Portugal.

1692	Edict of Toleration issued by K'ang-hsi, officially permitting Christian practices for the first time.
1715	Bull *Ex illa die*, forbidding any Roman Catholic concessions to Chinese beliefs.
1721	K'ang-hsi rejects the Bull and requires missionaries to make concessions.
1724	Christianity pronounced a heretical sect. Missionaries (other than astronomers) expelled. Persecutions of Christians continue throughout Yung-cheng's reign (1722–36).
1742	Papal Bull *Ex quo singulari*, finally and absolutely forbidding concessions (Benedict XIV).
1762	Jesuits expelled from Macao by the Portuguese.
1773	Society of Jesus disbanded. Emperor Ch'ien-lung (1736–95) retains ex-Jesuits in his service; 456 had worked in China since Xavier.
1783	Lazarist (secular) Mission commissioned to take over Roman Catholic interests in China.
1788	Lazarist Fr. Raux in charge of the Board of Astronomy. Other Lazarists fulfill previously Jesuit functions in the capital.

Education in China

The importance of education was recognized at least as far back as the early Chou dynasty. Confucius is the earliest individual teacher of whom we know, his curriculum containing such subjects as ethics, political theory, and the interpretation of the past. Perhaps he was the first to establish the view, current under the Empire, that learning from ancient texts was the ideal training for a scholar-official: He certainly set one other important precedent by accepting students on the basis of enthusiasm and ability to learn rather than of class or wealth. He is reported to have said, "Only one who bursts with eagerness do I instruct; only one who bubbles with excitement do I enlighten. If I hold up one corner (of an argument) and a man cannot come back to me with the other three, I do not continue the lesson."[1]

From Han times onward, intellectual ability was the only recognized way of obtaining an official post. The Han government opened some schools and the Imperial Academy, but the best way of testing ability had not yet been worked out. Recruitment to government service was usually on the recommendation of officials, supplemented by tests set by the Emperor. Local officials were sometimes instructed to look out for men with talents that were specially needed: Wang Mang (A.D. 9–23) called for, among others, astronomers, historians, mathematicians, musicians, etymologists, and herbalists.

The government of the T'ang exerted real control over a wider area and needed many more officials than had the Han. At the same time, the wider availability of books and the extra encouragement given to learning by both the Confucians and the Buddhists caused more men to aim at entering the civil service. The simple system of recommendation could no longer serve. Written examinations took its place and continued to be held regularly until the end of the Empire, the only serious interruption being under the Mongols. Competitors in the T'ang, who still had to have a patron, could choose their examination subject from several, including law, calligraphy, and arithmetic. In fact, most chose the classics, in which there was a one-in-ten pass rate: This compared with only one in a hundred in the other subjects. But those who gained the highest reputation were those who took and passed the section known as *chin-shih*, "presented scholars." Its papers were the hardest and included questions on the classics, politics, or current affairs and the composition of prose and poetry.

Significant educational changes also took place in the Sung

[1] *Analects*, VII/8; tr. A. Waley

dynasty. The most important was the substitution of a qualifying exam, the Prefectural, for the recommendation previously necessary. This meant that anyone could try for an
eventual *chin-shih* degree, which in time became the only
survivor of the T'ang examination categories. Records show
that some people actually did rise to positions of authority
from humble origins. More government schools and some
private academies were opened, though conditions of service
and low salaries caused a shortage of teachers and prevented
the whole of the official program from being carried out; and
in any case the cost of tuition and books put it beyond the
hopes of the majority. In general, however, the level of liter-
acy and the demand for books rose, and competition in the
metropolitan exams increased. Efforts were made to keep the
question papers objective and selection as free from corruption as possible, and the Emperor himself retested the successful *chin-shih* candidates before dividing them into classes.

In the Ming dynasty, central and local government was
made more complicated than ever before, and to match it the
education and examination systems became more detailed.
Question papers were almost entirely concerned with the
classics, and critics complained that successful parrot-like
repetition of these did not really prove that a man would make
a good minister of state. However, the intensive work required over several years in order to pass the *chin-shih* did at
least show that he could concentrate and persevere, and defenders of the system correctly pointed out that, however
inconsequentially, it did seem to pick out capable officials.
Those who felt that preparation for exams in state schools was
too narrowly specialized could go instead to a private academy, where there were generally better libraries and teachers
and sometimes a wider syllabus. Because they might consider
aspects of politics and philosophy that were not necessarily
acceptable to orthodox government Confucianism, these

academies sometimes became rallying centers for outspoken critics of the regime and so ran the risk of being closed down.

Primary education had to be arranged with private tutors. The academies and state schools offered only secondary education and dealt with entry procedure for the official exams. There were many of these, ranging from the initial county qualifying exam up to the final palace exam conducted by the Emperor in Peking. The tests were held at regular intervals of one to three years by important government officials and their staffs. The lowest attracted thousands of candidates in each county center, and the normal life of the town was disrupted during the period of the examination.

Success in one of the preliminary exams, especially in the prefectural capital, meant a great deal to the candidate and his family. It made him a local figure, exempted him from *corvée*, or forced labor, qualified him to teach and to help settle lawsuits, made him influential friends, and brought him gifts from less fortunate neighbors who suddenly wanted his patronage. It could also give him a scholarship to a state school and the chance to go on to the provincial and then the metropolitan exams. Admittedly, it was also possible to buy entry to the former, but in Ming times at least this was thought to be undignified.

The government paid the traveling expenses of each candidate going up to Peking. After receiving his question paper in the main examination hall, he was locked in a tiny brick cell, uniform with thousands of others that surrounded it in rows. Inside was a minimum of furniture and in one wall a window, through which a guard passed food, for the candidates might stay there for two or three days and nights. He might even die there: The psychological strain and extremes of climate were known to carry off some, especially of the more elderly candidates. In order to prevent favoritism, the answer papers were copied out and identified by a serial number before going to the examiners, so that anonymity was preserved. The results were published after a few days, and when the emperor had conducted the palace test of the successful candidates, they were graded in three classes. Those who passed the provincial and metropolitan exams stood a good chance of obtaining an official post, but they were only a small percentage of those who had taken them.

Corruption increased greatly during the Ch'ing period, but even so the East India Company, in trading contact with China, was sufficiently impressed with the ideal of impartial, public examinations to adopt a similar system for advancement in its own organization. This was in the early nineteenth century and it was the beginning in the West of what has become the widespread acceptance of public examinations for many different purposes.

Despite the efforts of Western missionaries and Chinese and Manchu reformers in the nineteenth century, and of Chiang Kai-shek's government in the twentieth, education remained the privilege of the few until the Communist period. Since the 1950's there has been a widespread extension of primary education, a slower but important increase in the provision of secondary education, and an opening of many specialized colleges of higher education.

Academic emphasis has been more on the sciences than on the arts, but since 1965 politics—notably the study and interpretation of *Quotations from Chairman Mao Tse-tung* (the "Little Red Book")—has become the main subject in the curriculum. Most schools closed for two years during the Cultural Revolution, and it proved difficult to reopen them. The upsetting of education may prove to have the most damaging long-term effects. Can a nation bent on swift industrial progress afford the suspension of general education and the disappearance of many of its teachers, or even the emphasis on Maoist politics, which have become the sole criterion for judging the suitability of a candidate for advancement? As in the Ming and Ch'ing periods, education has been narrowed to the study of prescribed books, and success depends on memory and conformity. The best men may shun such a system and refuse to serve the government. The result of this could be more serious to a developing power in the twentieth century than it was to a self-sufficient, slow-moving nation in the seventeenth.

Further Reading

Matteo Ricci's description of Ming China is translated by L. J. Gallagher, *China in the Sixteenth Century* (New York: Random, 1953, o.p.), and his biography told by V. Cronin, *The Wise Man from the West* (London: Hart-Davis, 1955). For a more detailed account of the Jesuit period, see H. G. Dunne, *Generation of Giants* (Notre Dame, Ind.: University of Notre Dame Press, 1962).

The stories that the Jesuits sent back to Europe made a considerable impression. They were, in particular, responsible for the vogue for Chinese works of art, architecture, garden planning, and so on described by Hugh Honour, *Chinoiserie* (New York: Dutton, 1962).

6

Europeans in Nineteenth-Century China

Imagine the effect on the American public if a rumor reached Washington that a tribe of Pacific Islanders, armed with more advanced nuclear weapons than our own, had captured California. The government would deny the story; few people would believe it; and even those who did would hardly think it was a serious threat to the whole nation. But suppose the story was found to be true. Suppose the Polynesians demanded the right to stay in the west and to travel farther east, to set up machinery of types unheard-of in this country, to flood our markets with cheap goods, and to put our people out of work. Suppose they told us we were ignorant, that our standards and institutions were pagan and out of date. Suppose they brought their own teachers to begin "brainwashing" us. Initial bewilderment would be followed by uproar. Only when the politicians had finished blaming one another would the debate begin on how to dislodge the invaders.

Such a thing could not happen now, and we should not press the analogy too far. But the world was a different place in the nineteenth century, and that was the kind of situation in which China found itself when the European nations, the United States, and Russia forced themselves onto its territory. The effect was as shattering to the well-established Chinese way of life as it would be to the American today.

Not that China had lacked opportunities to learn about the West and prepare for future relations. Its merchants had been dealing with East India Company men since the early eighteenth century. They must have had a good idea of the strength of foreign shipping. The Court itself had come across Western scientific and intellectual ability in its own European employees, the Jesuits. And in 1793 an embassy came to China from King George III. It consisted of ninety-five men, headed by Earl Macartney, and it offered the Manchus a chance to open talks on equal terms. What Macartney requested was an agreement providing for the exchange of resident ambassadors and the extension of Anglo-Chinese trade.

The Chinese received the embassy well and feted it, as they had always entertained parties bringing gifts of allegiance from vassal states. But they rejected the English proposals. They saw no reason to come to terms with the barbarians from the Western Ocean. Macartney summed up the rejection with an eye to the future:

> The Empire of China is an old, crazy first-rate man-of-war, which a fortunate succession of able and vigilant officers have contrived to keep afloat for these 150 years past, and to overawe their neighbors merely by her bulk and appearance, but whenever an insufficient man happens to have the command upon deck, adieu to the discipline and safety of the ship. She may perhaps not sink outright; she may drift some time as a wreck, and will then be dashed to pieces on the shore; but she can never be rebuilt on the old bottom.

In 1795 a Dutch embassy was received at Peking, and in 1816 the British were back again. This time they were led by Lord Amherst. With him were Sir George Staunton, who had been to China before as Earl Macartney's secretary and so had some knowledge of Chinese etiquette, and the Reverend Robert Morrison, a missionary from Macao who acted as principal interpreter.

Amherst fared even worse than Macartney had, not meeting the Emperor himself. The most fruitful outcome of the journey was the botanical information collected by the medical officer and naturalist to the British embassy, Clarke Abel. On the debit side, the party experienced sickness and extreme discomfort, insults, and even personal violence. Dr. Abel described the beginning of the long journey home from the court at Jehol:

> We reached the city of Peking at the close of day, stepped from our carts to steal a piece of its walls . . . and were hurried round them to its suburbs. It was dark when we entered them. A numberless mob again surrounded us, thrusting their lanterns, hanging from the ends of short staves, into the carts, to obtain a view of our faces. As we were not in a humor to indulge their curiosity, many of their lanterns coming into contact with our feet, were sacrificed to our irritability. Beyond the suburbs, we again got upon the paved road, and traveling along it at a fast trot, felt the sensation of continual dislocation and replacement in every joint of our bodies.

British interest in China was not deterred by the failure of the two embassies. Since relations could not be opened by diplomatic means, military operations were almost to be expected.

The first clash was over the extension of trade. Chinese imports of opium* from British India rose from 4,100 barrels in 1796 to 27,000 barrels in 1835. In 1834, the British Government ended the East India Company's monopoly and sent out a Superintendent of Trade, Napier, to organize facilities for merchants along the south China coast. The Chinese, however, were not willing to open other ports besides Canton to foreign ships. The government objected to the growing opium menace and sent a special commissioner to halt the trade. But neither he nor Captain Elliot, the new British Superintendent who had succeeded Napier on the latter's death, could control the Western merchants, and smuggling continued. It was an unsatisfactory state of affairs for both sides, and the British were prepared to use force to make China accept regular trade as between equal nations. A number of incidents occurred, and in November, 1839, a British fleet attacked the Chinese in the Pearl River and war broke out. A placard appearing in the streets of Canton in 1841 announced: "If we do not completely exterminate you pigs and dogs, we will not be manly Chinese."

The British Navy, with its superior armaments, quickly demolished the opposition. Most of the local Chinese marines were drug addicts and formed an ineffective fighting force. The government in Peking, not realizing the gravity of the situation, would not send its best troops. British casualties were slight, the highest in any single combat being three dead and twenty wounded. Afterward, in the Treaty of Nanking (August, 1842), Britain dictated its own terms. These included an indemnity* of $21 million, a maximum duty of only five per cent on imported foreign goods, the opening of five "treaty" ports on the southeast coast to merchants and foreign consuls, and the gift of Hong Kong* Island. Two years later, in a treaty with France, a clause was inserted to the effect that any future concession made by China to a Treaty Power could automatically be claimed by other foreign countries. This was known as the "most favored nation" clause.

The Court issued a proclamation saying: "Now that these

Rates of Freight, & Passage Money to and from

Canton, & Hongkong, Per Steamers

HANKOW & WHITE CLOUD.

The Steamers privileged to tow.

Alum,	per pecul	$0.80
Aniseed Oil,	case ½ pecul	0.30
Do. Star,	case do.	0.35
Do. Broken,	bale	0 30
Arsenic,	case	0.40
Beer,	4 doz. barrel or case	0.40
Do.	hhd.	1.25
Do.	kilderkin	0.75
Betel Nut,	pecul	0.12
Bicho-de-mer,	pecul	0.30
Bird's Nests,	pecul	1.00
Blankets,	bales 25 pairs	0.75
Do.	case 25 pairs	1.00
Do.	case 50 pairs	1.50
Bone Ware,	case	0.50
Brass Buttons,	case	0.52
Do. Leaves,	box	0.30
Do. Ware,	case ½, a 50	0 75
Brocades,	case	1.00
Butter,	cask	0.50
Cambrics,	case	0.50
Camphor,	pecul	0.25
Canvas,	bale	1.00
Cassia,	case ½ pecul	0.30
Do.	over 10 tons, per ton	1.50
Do. Oil,	case ½ pecul	0.50
Do. Twigs,	pecul	0.30
Cassia Buds,	case ½ pecul	0.30
Chair, Sedan,		2 00
Do., Bamboo extension,		0.50
Do., Rattan,	large	0 25
Do., Do.,	small	0.15
Do., Do., Pkge, of 2,		0.40
China-root,	pecul	0.20
China ware,	case	0.50
Cloves,	pecul	0.30
Cochineal,	case	1.00
Do.,	ceroon	1.00
Do.,	cask	2.00
Copper Cash,	pecul	0.15
Do. Sheathing & Yellow Metal,	case	1.50
Do. Nails,	cask	2 00
Do. do.,	keg	0.50
Cotton—Bombay,	bale	0.50
Do.,	half do	0.30
Bengal or Madras,	bale	0.40
Shanghae,	bale	0.40
Cotton Yarn,	bale	0.75
Cotton Goods,	case 50 pcs.	0.75
Do. Do.,	bale 50 pcs.	0.60
Do. Tweed,	large bale	1.00
Do.,	small do	0.60
American Drills,	bale 15 pcs	0.50
„ Jeans,	bale 20 pcs	0.60
„ Sheetings,	bale	0.60
Chintz,	case 0.60 a	0.75
Cigars,	case of 10,000	1.00
Cardamums,	case	0.50
Coral Beads,	case	0.75
Cornelians,	case	1.00
Carpet, (China)	bale	0.50
Copper Beads,	case	0.50
Damasks,	case	1.20
Emerald Green,	case	0.50
Fans,	case	0.50
Fire Carckers,	box	0 05
Do.	over 10 tons, per ton	1.50
Flour,	barrel	0.35
Do.	half-barrel	0.25
Furs,	casks	2.00
Feather's Kingfisher's,	case	1 00
Fish Maws,	per pecul	0 50
Ginseng,	hhd.	1 50
Do.,	cases 75 a	1.00
Do.,	puncheons	1.25
Do.,	barrel	0.75
Grasscloth,	case 25 a	0.75
Glass Bangles,	case	0.40
Do. Beads,	box	0.35
Glass Ware,	hhd.	2.00
Do.	case 50 a	1.00
Glue,	case ½ pecul	0 30
Gum, Myrrh,	pecul	0.30
Do. Olibanum,	pecul	0 20
Horse or Pony,		10.00
Hides, Buffalo,	bale pecul	0.20
Horns, Deer,	pecul	1.00
Do. Rhinoceros,	pecul	0 50
Iron,	pecul	0.15
Isinglass, Japan	pecul	0.50
Ivory,	pecul	0.75
Ivory, Ware,	case	0.75
Lacquered Ware,	case 50 a	1 00
Lead,	pecul	0 15
Linen,	case	0.40
Lead, White, Red, Yellow,	box	0.20
Lychees Dried,	case	0.25
Lung-ngan do	case	0.25
Musical boxes,	case	2.00
Matting for Tea, Bundle of 200		0.20
Musk,	on value, ½ per cent.	
Mushrooms,	case	0.40
Mother-o'Pearl Ware,	case	0.75
Marble Slabs, per box of 5 Slabs,		0.10
Do. do. 10 „		0 15
Matting,	roll	0.25
Do.,	over 10 tons, per ton	1 50
Muslins,	case	0.75
Nankeens,	case	0.30
Do.,	bale	0.25
Nutmegs,	pecul	0.50
Oil,	tub	1.00
Opium,	chest	2 00
Paper,	pecul	0 10
Pitch,	barrel	0.50
Preserves,	box	0.15
Do.,	say over 10 tons	1.50
Provisions, Salt,	barrel	0.50
Do.,	tierce	0.65
Prussian blue,	case	0.30
Putchuck,	pecul	0.30
Paper, Coloured,	case	0.35
Paper, Gilt,	case	0.40
Pearls,	on value ½ per cent	
Pearls, False,	case	0.50
Peel, Orange,	bale	0.50
Quicksilver,	flask ½ pecul	0.25
Do.,	flask 1 pecul	0.40
Rattans,	pecul	0.15
Rhubarb,	pecul	0.40
Rice,	pecul	0.15
Rosin,	barrel	0.40
Saltpetre,	pecul	0 25
Sandal Wood,	pecul	0.25

Plate 12. A page from the China Directory, *1864.*
The distance between Hong Kong and Canton is 91 miles.

foreigners have been pacified, a border dispute must not be allowed to break out again." Antiforeign feeling flared temporarily, but the opium trade, which had never really stopped, went on growing. So did trading in other Western goods, such as wool and cotton.

Too much money left the country, and too much of what remained found its way into the pockets of corrupt officials. The government was too poor to be able to help the large areas suffering from floods and droughts since 1821. Millions of Chinese were starving, and during the 1850's five major rebellions broke out. The most serious was the Taiping (Great Peace) rising. Its leader, Hung Hsiu-ch'üan, claimed to be the brother of Jesus Christ. He proclaimed a social reform program based on elements of Christianity. His promises, however, were greater than his organizing ability, and his own moral standards not up to those he expected of his followers —he himself had sixty concubines. The peasantry at first welcomed his armies, which had swept as far north as Tientsin by 1853. Then, at the crucial moment, support for the rebels failed. The government forces, professing Confucianism, gave practical relief to war-damaged villages. The Taipings, professing Christianity and promising much, did nothing except cause devastation. By 1864, the rebellion was under control.

After 1860, British and French troops helped the imperial army. In the midst of its domestic troubles the government had been compelled to sign two new international treaties. One of the treaty ports, Canton, had not been opened to foreigners since 1842, and the Western powers had long felt that the Nanking agreement needed general revision.

In February, 1856, a French missionary was killed in Kwangsi. In October, the Chinese authorities detained a boat sailing from Hong Kong under the British flag, carrying twelve Chinese pirates. These two events gave the British and French the excuse they needed for a new display of military

force. They captured Canton and their navies threatened
Peking. In 1858 and 1860, the treaties of Tientsin and Peking
were signed. It was in European interests that the Manchus
should remain in power to carry out their obligations under
them. Among these were an indemnity of four million taels
($7 million), freedom of travel for foreigners, including mis-
sionaries, and the gift of Kowloon. A total of sixteen ports
were now open for trade.

The Chinese began to consider the weakness of their position
for the first time. They were obviously unable to drive the
Westerners out by force of arms and could no longer even
confine them to the ports. The conclusion was reached, not
without bitter opposition, that they should "learn the strong
techniques of the barbarians in order to control them" (Wei
Yuan, 1794–1856).

So began the modernization of China. It was stimulated by
three politicians who came into prominence after fighting the
Taiping rebels. Their names were Tseng Kuo-fan, Li Hung-
chang and Tso Tsung-t'ang. They are the greatest figures in
nineteenth-century Chinese history. They were the chief
financiers of a program of industrial building between the
1860's and 1890's. They built ships and railways; armament
factories; ironworks; coal mines; flour, paper, and textile
mills; and much more. Europeans and Americans cooperated
and gave technical advice.

If the Chinese Government and people had been united in
their attempts to modernize, if there had been a national
economic plan, China could have achieved the success Japan
was soon to have. In fact, China had the better chance, for the
Western powers were more ready to help it than Japan. Yet
whereas the Japanese set about the task with whole-hearted
enthusiasm and thoroughness, the Chinese were too concerned
with hanging on to their past. They lacked the necessary sense
of purpose and did not see what a golden opportunity they

had to make a new and potentially great nation. They sent students to England and America; in Peking's Progressive School they trained interpreters and followed a Western syllabus; they installed modern machinery and learned Western skills. But their efforts were half-hearted. The government hindered rather than helped: When a company made a profit, the government representatives on its board of directors were more likely to pocket a large share than allow it to be put back into the company. Their minds were not on competition in the twentieth century, as were the minds of the Japanese; they were on finding the quickest way of driving out the intruders so that the traditional Chinese way of life could be resumed. It was a failure from which China is still trying to recuperate.

The inhabitants of the seaports again became accustomed to the sight of foreign faces. Merchants from almost every European country moved in, along with Americans, Russians, Indians, Siamese, Japanese, and Peruvians. Diplomatic staff came too, not to mention teachers, doctors, journalists, scientists, engineers, and tourists. This was the best opportunity ever to have arisen for Westerners and Chinese to get together and learn to understand each other, but it was lost. Apart from working hours, when cooperation was unavoidable, the foreigners generally remained aloof from the Chinese. A notable exception was Sir Robert Hart, an Irishman who became Inspector-General of the Chinese Imperial Maritime Customs Service* and was an influential adviser to the Chinese Government.

Educated Chinese likewise regarded the foreigners with contempt, an attitude that was less defensible in the nineteenth century than it would have been under the T'ang or Sung. The great empire had visibly decayed, roads and canals had fallen into disrepair; towns were dirtier; the countryside was infested with bandits and the coasts with pirates. The prosperity of the past had gone. So too had the high standards of

honesty and morality that had once been the mark of Confucianism. The following description comes from an anony-
mous English work written in 1840:

> They plunder and cheat each other from the highest to the
> lowest; never allowing an opportunity to escape, when detec-
> tion may be avoided; for neither human suffering nor life are
> regarded by those in authority, when the infliction of the one,
> or the destruction of the other, can be made subservient to the
> acquisition of wealth or power. They will enrich themselves
> by the acquisition of their neighbors' property; and should they
> be detected, the punishment would be stayed, upon the pay-
> ment of a certain sum: For, so corrupt are the streams of justice,
> that even the punishment of death may be compounded for.
> They are wholly destitute of shame; and when punishments are
> inflicted, the pain with which they are accompanied is all that
> is regarded. . . . "Our rulers," say they, "want money, and
> care little about the means by which it is obtained. If you know
> this, you know the principles and practice of our government."

This author happens to be hostile to the Chinese, whom he
calls "the most artful, sly, idle, and cowardly [people] in
existence." But there was certainly some substance to what he
wrote. It was borne out by Robert Douglas, a Professor of
Chinese at King's College, London, in 1887:

> The constitution of the civil service renders it next to impos-
> sible that any office-holder can be clean-handed in the European
> sense. The salaries awarded are low out of all proportion to the
> necessary expenses pertaining to the offices to which they are
> apportioned, and the consequence is that, in some way or other,
> the officials are compelled to make up the deficiency from the
> pockets of those subject to them. . . .
>   Flogging with bamboos on the hind part of the thighs or
> between the shoulders, beating the jaws with thick pieces of
> leather or the ankles with a stick are some of the preliminary

tortures applied to witnesses or culprits who refuse to give the
evidence expected of them. Further refinements of cruelty are
reserved for hardened offenders, by means of which infinite
pain, and often permanent injury, are inflicted on the knee
joints, fingers, ankles, etc. (R. K. Douglas, *China*, 1887.)

For the instruction and entertainment of the British public,
many books were published about China and its people. They
were often very good, and they helped to counterbalance the
anti-China propagandists. Although they sometimes overcon-
centrated on the curiosities, they also gave accurate information about more serious matters, such as religious beliefs,
education, history, and government. The following are examples taken from these books, written by nineteenth-century
Europeans who had been to China:

The test of my Chinese disguise awaited me at Pihkwan, which
we reached at 3 P.M. My traps were landed first, and then I
set about attiring myself in the cabin in the summer costume of
the country—a broad-brimmed straw hat, a grasscloth jacket,
calico trousers, brand-new sash, gay blue garters, light straw
shoes, a fan in one hand, and umbrella in the other, and a
rough handkerchief up the sleeve. Thus accoutred I landed.
But I had scarely set my foot on the bank when a voice near
me shouted out in the patois of the place, "Hie-ya! Here's an
Englishman!" (W. C. MILNE, *Life in China*, 1861.)

It is a prevalent notion that an eclipse is occasioned by some
monster 'dragon', attempting to swallow up the sun or the
moon. . . . The result of such absurdity is that, during an
eclipse, there is an incessant din of gongs, drums, horns, cym-
bals, pipes, fifes, etc., along with the letting off of crackers and
popguns; all this hurly-burly being kept up to frighten away
the devouring beast. They likewise shoot arrows at the sun or
moon. . . . The priests are particularly religious on the occasion,
and go through all the ceremony of bowing, kneeling, chanting,

etc.; and in their private residences the people are observing a similar farce, imploring the animal to pity their dilemma and spare the greater and lesser lights. When the eclipse is over they believe they have been successful in their entreaties. *(Ibid.)*

One may say, in fact, that all China is an immense library; for inscriptions, sentences, moral precepts, are found in every corner written in letters of all colors and all sizes. The façades of the tribunals, the pagodas, the public monuments, the signs of the shops, the doors of houses, the interior of the apartments, the corridors, all are full of fine quotations from the best authors. Teacups, vases, fans, are so many selections of poems, often chosen with much taste and prettily printed. A Chinese has no need to give himself much trouble in order to enjoy the finest productions of his country's literature. (ABBÉ HUC, *The Chinese Empire*, 1855).

The literary examinations are, like everything else, degenerating and falling into decay. They have no longer the grave, earnest, impartial character that was doubtless impressed on them at the time of their institution. The corruption which has spread through everything without exception in China has also found its way among both examiners and examined. The rules that ought to be observed in the examinations are extremely stringent, with a view to prevent any fraud, and discover the true merit of the candidate; but, by certain financial methods, a way has been found to neutralize the effects of these precautions. A rich man can always find out beforehand the subjects proposed for the various compositions; and, what is worse, even the suffrages of the judges are sold to the highest bidder. *(Ibid.)*

In their diversions, the Chinese have much of that childish character which distinguishes other Asiatics. . . . The mind under despotism has few of those calls for exertion, among the bulk of the people, which in free states give it manly strength and vigor. Bearing no part in public transactions, and living in uninterrupted peace, the uniform insipidity of their existence is relieved by any, even the most frivolous and puerile, amusements. . . . My attention was drawn by several old Chinese, some of whom had gray beards, and nearly all of them huge goggling spectacles. A few were chirruping and chuckling to singing birds, which they carried in bamboo cages, or perched on a stick; others were catching flies to feed the birds; the remainder of the party seemed to be delightedly employed in flying paper kites, while a group of boys were gravely looking on, and regarding these innocent occupations of their seniors with the most serious and gratified attention. (J. F. Davis, *The Chinese*, 1851.)

The vice of opium-smoking has long since become a gigantic obstacle to the welfare and prosperity of this people. The consumption of opium is rapidly on the increase in the city (Foochow) as well as in other parts of the Empire, and its ravages are becoming more manifest and more awful. Shops where the drug is offered for sale are becoming more and more common. Its unhappy victims are becoming more and more numerous. The nation is becoming poorer and poorer. . . . It is a sad, sad thought, that the principals, partners, employees, and agents of a few foreign mercantile firms in this heathen land annually realize a far greater amount of money from their traffic in this drug than is annually contributed by the millions of their pious fellow-countrymen at home for the Christianization of the Chinese! (The Rev. Justus Doolittle, *Social Life of the Chinese*, 1865.)

Their pillows are oblong cubes of bamboo, or other hard material. For the maintenance of the existing fashions of female hairdressing, this kind of pillow is essential to women at least, whose hair, which is only dressed at intervals of days, and which is kept in its grotesque shapes by the abundant use of bandoline, would be crushed and disfigured if lain upon for a moment. Women, therefore, who make any pretense of following the fashion are obliged to sleep at night on their backs, resting the nape of the neck on the pillow, thus keeping the head and hair free from contact with anything. (R. K. Douglas, *op. cit.*)

Finally, compare these two assessments of the Chinese character. The first is by Sir Robert Hart and the second by a missionary, the Rev. George Smith.

They are well behaved, law-abiding, intelligent, economic, and industrious; they can learn anything and do anything; they are punctiliously polite, they worship talent, and they believe in right so firmly they scorn to think it requires to be supported or enforced by might . . . they possess and practice an admirable system of ethics, and they are generous, charitable, and fond of good works.

The universal practice of lying, and suspicion of dishonesty between man and man; the unblushing lewdness of old and young; the full, unchecked torrent of human depravity borne along in its tempestuous channel, and inundating the social system with the overflowing of ungodliness, proves the existence of a kind and degree of moral degradation among people, of which an adequate conception can rarely be formed.

Missionaries

One class of foreigner against whom the charge of remaining aloof could not be leveled was the missionary.

In the opening years of the nineteenth century the Roman Catholic Church in China was weak. Although its members were to be found in every province, their total number did not exceed 250,000. This hardly increased between 1800 and 1840. Partly to blame for this was the political situation in Europe: The upheavals following the French Revolution and the Napoleonic wars severely curtailed the opportunities for French, Italian, Spanish, and Portuguese priests to leave for the East. In 1810, there were only thirty-one Roman Catholic missionaries in the whole of China. More to blame was the attitude of the Chinese Government. Fearful of the danger from secret societies, it classified Christianity as a heretical sect and forbade its dissemination. Serious persecutions took place on a nationwide scale in 1805 and 1811, and several other local ones occurred before 1840. Chinese and European clergy alike were executed or exiled. They made no excuses, for they knew they were breaking the law of the land by preaching. Europeans were happy to associate themselves with the Chinese in this way. The list of martyrs shows that the Church was lucky not to have been exterminated altogether.

Meanwhile, Protestant missionaries from Europe and America were moving into the field. First to come was Robert Morrison, of the London Missionary Society, who arrived in 1807. He and his colleagues were only allowed into the small foreign quarter in Canton, which was then the only open port. This and the Portuguese-occupied territory of Macao were made their centers of operation. Even in the latter they worked quietly for fear of provoking the authorities. They did not set out to make converts. In fact, they baptized fewer than one hundred Chinese before 1840. They began preparing the ground by opening schools and hospitals and prepared the seed itself by translating the Bible and other Christian literature into Chinese. Some of this was distributed secretly along the coast.

After the Treaty of Nanking, Christian missionaries, both Roman Catholic and Protestant, were able to extend their activities to the four newly opened ports, Amoy, Foochow, Ningpo and Shanghai. Protestants were also glad to move to more secure headquarters on the British island of Hong Kong. Furthermore, an imperial edict of 1844 proclaimed that missionaries found outside the treaty ports were no longer to be tried by Chinese authorities but were to be taken back to their

own consuls in the ports. Christians hailed this as a pronounce-
ment of religious toleration, but in some cases their joy was
short-lived. Either the edict was not made known to all local
authorities, or some of them ignored it. Missionaries making
unauthorized journeys into the interior discovered this to their
cost. Certainly, some were escorted back to the coast un-
harmed, but others died from the hardships inflicted on them
en route, and elsewhere executions continued as before. In
1855, a French Lazarist priest with fourteen years' experience
in China, the Abbé Huc, wrote:

> China is far from being open; and whatever may be said, we
> believe that our missions have very little hope there. . . . Their
> situation is not in the least ameliorated; they are, as they were
> before, at the mercy of the Mandarins,* who persecute them,
> pillage them, throw them into prison, torture them, and send
> them to die in exile just as easily as if there were no representa-
> tive of France in the Empire, and no French ships of war on
> her coasts.

From Europe, however, the missionary prospect seemed
brighter. More organizations sent workers. Among the Roman
Catholics were Jesuits, Franciscans, Dominicans, and Lazarists.
British Protestant societies included the London Missionary
Society, the Church Missionary Society, and the Methodist
and Presbyterian Societies; and there were many others from
Europe and America. The number of charitable institutions
increased, even in the inland provinces. The Protestants, however, restricted their activities mainly to the treaty ports and
so escaped the reprisals that Roman Catholics still suffered.
The total of Chinese Christians slowly began to rise.

One further boost to the missionary cause was yet to come.
The Treaty of 1860 not only legalized the presence of Roman
Catholics in the provinces but also opened the door to Protes-
tants for the first time. Implied, though not explicitly stated,

was the concession that missionaries might own property outside the treaty ports. And most important of all, a guarantee was made that Christians, both European and Chinese, would now be protected instead of persecuted.

The Christians did not hesitate to exploit their rights. Numbers of missionaries and converts rose faster. Of the former, China was served by some 750 Roman Catholics, mostly French, by 1895. In the same year the China Inland Mission accounted for 600 out of the whole Protestant force of about 1,400 missionaries. This compared with a figure of 189 in 1864, the year before the mission's foundation. Chinese converts to Protestantism are estimated to have been about 55,000 in 1893, and those to the Roman Church at about 530,000 in 1897.

It would be misleading to compare the progress of the respective churches on the basis of these figures, or even to judge the influence of Christianity as a whole. For one thing, Chinese who had infringed their own laws often became "converts" simply to obtain the protection of Western missionaries and consuls, guaranteed to Christians in 1860. For another, conversion to Christianity did not always satisfy the Chinese that they must renounce their beliefs in Confucianism, Taoism, or Buddhism. They might pretend to do so, but this was frequently out of sympathy for the missionary, not from conviction. More "Christians" did not necessarily mean a significant increase in the Christian way of life, nor a decline in the influence of native Chinese beliefs. It is only fair to add, however, that many genuine and lasting converts were made, and that to many Chinese Christianity really did mean a change of life and salvation, at least from the torments of opium addiction.

The influence of Christianity is best seen not from statistics but from the history of the whole Chinese nation toward the end of the century. It was, as we have seen, a period of turmoil

when the Chinese were deeply divided over how best to meet
the challenge of the West. This challenge was presented not
only by weapons and machinery but also by new spiritual and
intellectual concepts that threatened to undermine the whole
structure of Chinese society. Some of the teachings of the
missionaries were unheard-of and unacceptable to the Chinese.
For example, they could not understand why they needed to
be forgiven for behavior that mere foreigners called "sinful."
Neither could they accept much of the dogmatism characteristic of nineteenth-century missionaries.

China benefited from Western schools and hospitals and
its scholars broadened their minds with translations of Western books, but aspects of the missionary work and approach
aroused hostility. There were the orphanages, for instance.
The Chinese peasants were very poor. Their families were
often too large to support, especially after a bad harvest. In
these circumstances, it was not uncommon for some of the
babies, usually the girls, to be sold or abandoned. This was
the accepted procedure, and the Chinese did not appreciate the
action of the missionaries in collecting and caring for these
children. Wild rumors circulated about their real motives. It
was said that they wanted their eyes and hearts for evil practices, and so the children would die. Very often, of course, the
babies were so neglected by the time they were found by the
missionaries that they soon did die, and this added strength
to the popular stories.

The missionaries could have helped their own cause by
informing themselves better about Chinese customs and beliefs. Yet few of them took the trouble to find out and work
upon such aspects of the three Chinese religions as were common to Christianity. They simply condemned them as idol-
atry and paganism and talked of "conquering" them. The
editor of the Tientsin *Chinese Times*, Alexander Michie,
wrote in 1891:

What must strike anyone on reading a series of missionary records, such for instance as the proceedings of the conferences held at Shanghai, is the extreme subjectiveness of their utterances, in word and writing, and the corresponding absence of objectiveness. Their thoughts are full of themselves, their doctrines, their organization, their methods, their efforts, their disappointments, their piety, their charity, their humility and self-effacement; while the condition of the Chinese mind and conscience is passed over with some threadbare commonplaces, as if no account need be taken of that great factor in the problem!

He quoted the Rev. J. Hudson Taylor, speaking at the 1890 conference, as saying: "The title of his paper [Dr. Martin's *Plea for Toleration*] is one that cannot be discussed by any Protestant body."

The Protestant societies might do better, Michie suggested, if they were to standardize and simplify their teachings. As it was, they only confused the Chinese with the variations in their beliefs and practices, some of which were, to say the least, difficult to understand:

A lady, fresh perhaps from some theological seminary, propounds for "Chinese women"—women who, on the testimony of another experienced and keen-witted missionary lady, are unable to grasp the simplest abstract idea—a scheme of divinity so elaborate that if the salvation of our bishops were made conditional on their mastering it the majority of their lordships would have sorrowfully to accept the alternative.

Only a tiny proportion of the Chinese people found that Christianity supplanted their own religions. Many who might have adopted it in addition to the other three, were put off by its assertion of superiority and by the fact that it was a foreign religion, backed with the legal power of foreign consuls and foreign weapons. The Chinese, despite their attempts at Westernization, were still hostile to foreigners. Murders and riots involving missionaries and Chinese Christians continued to take place. The most infamous was at Tientsin on June 21, 1870, when a French consul and twelve missionaries were killed. The consuls were not too well-disposed toward their own missionaries, who were often an embarrassment to them, but in their own interests they were obliged to offer them the protection to which they were entitled.

If missionaries were the prime offenders in aggravating racial tension, they were not the only ones to feel the effects. Michie wrote:

> The universal tendency for mobs to gather around stray foreigners, the rough way they press upon travelers even into the rooms of their inn, the volleys of foul epithets and even of clods and stones always ready to descend on the slightest suggestion, seem to betray a substratum of ill-feeling covered by a very thin crust of civility.

As missionaries spread, he went on, so did the hatred of all foreigners. It was whipped up by secret societies and became more intense after China's defeat in a war with Japan in 1895. As the foreign powers, notably Britain, France, Germany, Russia, and Japan, scrambled unashamedly for territory and influence, China's humiliation was complete.

One of the secret societies, the Boxer, took the lead in arousing opposition. A series of attacks on foreigners in many parts of the country culminated in June, 1900, in the attack on those in Peking and Tientsin. With encouragement from the Empress Tz'u-hsi, sieges were mounted. The 600 foreign residents of Peking were confined with 1,000 Chinese Christian refugees within the British Legation, an area measuring only 700 yards by 200 yards. The Empress declared a state of war between China and the powers, which, fortunately for many missionaries, the most influential provincial governors decided to ignore.

Against all the odds, the beleaguered foreigners held out. They were outnumbered and their weapons and ammunition were scanty. So were their medical supplies and food. The Chinese attacked with cannon, machine-guns, rifles, and incendiary arrows. All hope of survival seemed lost when, on August 14, an international relief force arrived from Tientsin. Resistance from the Boxers and imperial troops collapsed, and the Empress and her Court fled from Peking.

The siege had lasted fifty-five days. It had cost the powers a total of sixty-four killed and one hundred and fifty wounded, but it provided them with another opportunity for exacting an enormous indemnity, this time of $333 million. It was the beginning of the end for the Ch'ing dynasty, which was overthrown in 1911.

Further Reading

Macartney's own entertaining account of his mission has been edited by J. L. Cranmer-Byng, *An Embassy to China, Lord Macartney's Journal 1793–4* (London: Longmans, Green, 1962). For further reading see:

Arthur Waley, *The Opium War Through Chinese Eyes* (Stanford, Cal.: Stanford University Press, 1968); Peter Fleming, *The Siege at Peking* (New York: Harper & Row, 1959)—the dramatic story of the Boxer rising, expertly told, with photographs and eyewitness accounts; and Kenneth S. Latourette, *A History of Christian Missions in China* (New York: Paragon, n.d.).

Chinese objections to the teachings of the Christian missionaries are outlined by Charles P. Fitzgerald, *The Birth of Communist China* (New York: Praeger, 1966).

7

An American in Communist China

The revolution that overthrew the Ch'ing dynasty was the last of a series of attempted insurrections to take place in the early years of the twentieth century. These were particularly inspired by three would-be reformers, K'ang Yu-wei, Liang Ch'i-ch'ao, and Sun Yat-sen. The last named was the most active in stirring up anti-Manchu feeling, although he was in America when the final *coup* was staged in 1911.

To replace the imperial system of government, a republic was established. It was not a success. Individuals in the National Assembly were more concerned for their own interests than those of the country. They would not work together to give China what it needed most of all, a united voice to speak with strength to the other nations of the world. In 1917 China was persuaded to enter World War I, a far from unanimous decision on its part. The Kuomintang (KMT), or Nationalist Party, withdrew to Canton and set up a rival government there. In 1921, Sun Yat-sen accepted its nomination as President.

Parts of the Shantung Peninsula had been on lease to Germany since 1898, and when the war was over China expected that they would be returned. Certainly the Treaty of Versailles took them away from the Germans, but it gave them to the Japanese, who had the most obvious designs on Chinese territory. Feelings ran high in China against all foreign powers except one: Russia.

Russia, it was pointed out, had not indulged in the opium trade, had not sent missionaries to upset Chinese villages, had not carried men away to the West Indian slave plantations, as the Western powers had done. In 1920, Russia voluntarily surrendered its extraterritorial* rights to China and its share of the Boxer indemnity, another sign of sympathy with China. Moreover, Russia had recently succeeded in doing what China seemed to have failed to accomplish, namely, to replace a despotism with a government genuinely interested in the ordinary people. Chinese intellectuals were naturally attracted by Russian propaganda. Groups studied Marxism in the cities of Europe, Russia, and China, and in July, 1921, the Chinese Communist Party (CCP) was founded.

In its early years, the Party worked in association with the KMT in southern China. Their aims were the same: nationalism (to end foreign intrusion on Chinese soil and to compel respect from other countries) and socialism (to turn out the Peking government and to make life easier for the Chinese peasant under one of his own choosing). The republic had degenerated into warlordism; that is to say, overpowerful subjects had built up private armies, divided the land into their own spheres of influence, and now ruled the countryside in a tyrannical way, as bad as feudalism at its worst.

In the summer of 1926, the KMT and the Communist Party moved north with an army of 100,000 men. In early October

they captured Hankow, and on March 22, 1927, Shanghai fell
to them. The Communists were not elated by this success. Sun
Yat-sen had died in 1925 and had been succeeded by Chiang
Kai-shek. The Communists believed that Chiang's ambitions
were more like those of the warlords than those of Sun's
socialism. The cracks between the CCP and the KMT became
too deep to paper over. In April, 5,000 Communists were
executed in Shanghai and the alliance broke up. What had
been at best suspicious cooperation between Nationalists and
Communists now turned into open and bitter hostility. The
KMT swept northward and took Peking in June, 1928.
Chiang announced that he had reunited China. He discounted
the activities of the Communists and of those warlords whom
he had not encountered.

Over a period of three years the Communists, with Mao
Tse-tung prominent, organized uprisings in a number of
selected towns. None was successful. Of an estimated Party
membership of 50,000 in 1927, all but 10,000 had been mas-
sacred by the end of 1928. In the last insurrection, at Chang-
sha in August, 1930, 2,000 Communists died. Chiang Kai-shek
could well afford to discount their activities.

He reckoned without the psychological, military, and organizing genius of such Communists as Mao and Chou En-lai.
They and other Communists who had held high office under
the KMT/CCP alliance escaped the massacres and regrouped
the remains of their party in a safe area, around Jui-chin in
Kiangsi. Far from being defeated, they began to run the district themselves along Communist lines, and by 1934 the
Kiangsi Soviet,* as it was called, had expanded to include two
million people.

The Long March

Between November, 1930, and June, 1932, Nationalist armies
attacked the Soviet four times. The fifth campaign, mounted

in October, 1933, began to strangle the Communist base. A year later, the evacuation of the area was ordered. On the night of October 15, 1934, a column of more than 120,000 men, women, and children escaped through a gap in the enemy encirclement and headed west.

Some of the marchers were old, many were in their teens, and some were only ten or eleven. They had been supplied with food and weapons, but they were not prepared for a long march. For one thing, their clothing and footwear were quite inadequate. Most of them walked, because the pack

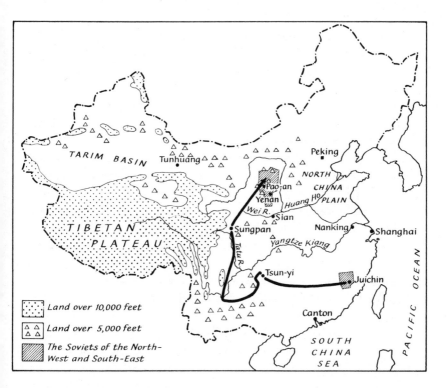

Map 6. The Long March

animals were loaded down with machine tools, printing machines, sewing machines, and extra weapons. The column was led by the Red Army, and spirits were high.

In the early days they learned from their mistakes. They were hampered by too much baggage and they marched on too obvious a line, straight toward the Yangtze. KMT armies killed 4,000, and as the Reds entered Kweichow Province they found all approaches to the river blocked. For four months they maneuvered. Eventually they captured the Governor's palace at Tsunyi, and there Mao was elected Chairman of the national Communist Party and outlined his plans for the next stage of the march.

As the main force moved southwest into the rugged province of Yunnan, with its towering mountains, deep gorges, and thick forests, a Red Army battalion hurried on ahead toward the Yangtze. There were only two possible crossing points, and the Reds tricked the Nationalists into thinking that they were making for the northern one, at Leng-kai. The Nationalists burned all the boats and sat down on the northern bank to wait. The Reds never arrived. They raced instead to the southern one, at Chouping. Here the garrison was not so alert. The boats were drawn up on the northern bank. When the Reds arrived they put on captured KMT uniforms and forced a local official to shout across the river for a boat for some "government" soldiers. It came, and carried back enough Reds to seize the unprepared guard post. It took nine days to ferry the whole expedition across, but it was two days more before the pursuing Nationalists arrived on the south bank.

The marchers now turned north and penetrated the thick jungle of western Szechwan, the home of the hostile Lolo peoples. Their hostility, however, turned to cooperation as they were persuaded that they and the Reds were fighting a common enemy, the "White" Chinese. Some of them actually joined the Communists as they headed toward yet another danger, a torrential tributary of the Yangtze called the Tatu River.

Luck seemed to be with them, for on the south bank they found a boat, brought across by the garrison commander to visit his relations and carelessly left unattended. Once again a vanguard armed with machine-guns crossed and put the Whites to flight. Then they began to row their comrades across. But the river rose and prevented quick progress. Nationalist troops would soon be on the spot. Their bombers had already located it.

The operation had to be abandoned and the Reds set out, some on the north bank and some on the south, toward the only other crossing point. This was an old iron-chain suspension bridge some four hundred *li* to the west. It had once been planked over, but half the planks had been taken up, leaving fifty yards of bare chains swinging hundreds of feet above the racing stream. The bridge was defended by a machine-gun post, and the Reds had to cross it or be trapped.

Thirty volunteers were chosen, and under a covering hail of gunfire they began to swing their way across the sixteen exposed chains. Enemy guns opened fire and some were hit. Yet somehow, by some miracle, others escaped the bullets and lobbed hand grenades into the defenses. The Nationalists tried in vain to set fire to the bridge, and then they fled. To add to their panic, the Red forces already on the north bank arrived to attack them from the flank.

Moving north again, the column left the subtropical region and struggled up 16,000 feet onto the freezing eastern end of the Tibetan Plateau. After 4,000 miles, the fighting, physical exhaustion, and exposure to great extremes of climate had taken their toll. In August, 1935, only 30,000 were still on the march.

One more major obstacle confronted them. Turning north-eastward, they faced the Sungpan grasslands. This is bleak, desolate marshland. Vegetation is sparse, natural food and drinking water nonexistent. Bushes provide the only shelter from the almost continual rain. The Reds captured neighboring tribesmen to guide them across the only causeway, yet in ten agonizing days they lost some 20,000 comrades and many animals, victims of either hunger, exposure, or drowning in the swamp.

The end of the long march was now in sight. Natural barriers had been overcome. Only KMT forces stood between the Communists and their destination, and these could be defeated by guerrilla tactics: It had become almost a routine procedure. On October 20, 1935, the Long March ended. The weary remnants, less than 20,000 of the original 120,000, still including some children, made contact with the Soviet of the northwest and went to ground in the safety of the Shensi Mountain caves.

They had covered more than 6,000 miles, equal to twice the width of the United States. In a year's heavy marching and fighting they had had one hundred days' rest, fifty-six of which were taken at one stretch, up in the mountains of Szechwan. They had crossed eighteen mountain ranges, twenty-four rivers, and wild, uncharted areas where no Chinese had been before. They had fought successfully against natural hazards and the opposition of Chiang Kai-shek, ten different warlords, and several aboriginal tribes. They had completed one of the epics of human history. They had also surrounded themselves with legends of invincibility and had won many converts to Communism.

Edgar Snow

Early in June, 1936, a special correspondent of the *New York Sun* and the London *Daily Herald* arrived by train in Sian.

He was an American. His name was Edgar Snow. Outwardly, his presence in Sian provoked no comment, but in fact the circumstances surrounding his journey were dramatic. He was going where no correspondent had been before—behind the Red lines, into the Northwest Soviet. He carried a letter of introduction to no less a person than Mao Tse-tung himself, written in invisible ink. He did not know who had written it, a Red agent somewhere in Peiping. All that mattered was that it had been procured for him by a Chinese friend. Now, on reaching Sian, Snow was to go to the Guest Hostel and await further instructions.

The contact was duly made, and early one morning a heavy army truck rolled through the gates of Sian. Inside were the usual complement of soldiers, and Edgar Snow. The former wore the uniforms of the crack Tungpei, or Northeastern Army, which Chiang Kai-shek had withdrawn from Manchuria when Japan seized its capital in September, 1931. Its task now was to exterminate the Communists in Shensi, while the League of Nations settled the dispute with Japan. The army was bitter at not being allowed to fight the Japanese. Many of the soldiers sympathized with the Reds and despised Chiang.

In the afternoon of the following day, the truck reached Yenan. Here the road came to an end. This too was the last town under Nationalist control. Beyond lay Red China. Less than a year before, the marchers had struggled into hiding in this region utterly exhausted, but much had happened in a few months. Under the direction of Mao and Chou, the Soviet, which had first been established in Shensi in 1933, quickly became a unit covering the whole of northern Shensi and eastern Kansu, about the size of England. It governed itself efficiently and defiantly proclaimed its hostility to the Japanese and its opposition to the policies of Chiang Kai-shek. As Edgar Snow was to see, life for the Chinese in the north-

west was being transformed from drudgery and slavery into
something honorable and exciting.

In Yenan Edgar Snow found a man with a donkey who
would lead him past the last sentry and into Communist territory. He later wrote:

> For four hours we followed a small winding stream and did
> not see any sign of human life. There was no road at all, but
> only the bed of the stream that rushed swiftly between high
> walls of rock, above which rose swift hills of loess.* It was the
> perfect setting for the blotting out of a too-inquisitive foreign
> devil. A disturbing factor was the muleteer's frequently ex-
> pressed admiration of my cowhide shoes.

Snow need not have worried. Wherever he went during his
four months' stay with the Reds, he was treated with the
utmost friendliness and helpfulness.

His guide left him at the first village they came to. The
chief of the local Poor Peoples' League gave him a meal and
some Soviet money and arranged for a fresh companion to
escort him to An-tsai. This was a cave village, improvised in
the mountainsides years before when the original settlement
was destroyed by flooding. Here Snow hoped to meet Mao
Tse-tung.

Mao, as it happened, had gone, but Chou En-lai was there,
and Snow obtained his first interview with one of the most
"wanted" men in China. Several times he noted with surprise
that the Red leaders, men with enormous prices on their heads,
walked the streets of the Shensi villages with no elaborate
security precautions. Nor were their dress or living quarters
in any way ostentatious: They understood how the people
felt about things, because they lived like them. For their part,
the people respected and trusted them. Such close association
between commoners and officials was unheard of in Chinese

history. It was largely responsibile for the zestful, crusading spirit that Snow encountered everywhere in Red areas. For the first time, he saw people in China who were actively happy.

Chou En-lai gave him *carte blanche* to go where he pleased but also prepared a three-month tour for him to follow should he so desire. He sent him first to the Red capital, Pao-an, and radioed word ahead that he was coming. There was a radio school in Pao-an, from which the Communists maintained secret communications with all the major Chinese cities. They used equipment captured from the Nationalists.

In Pao-an, Snow was welcomed as a guest of the "Foreign Office," and very shortly he became the first foreign reporter ever to interview the Chairman of the Chinese Soviet Republic, Mao Tse-tung. He described him as "a gaunt, rather Lincolnesque figure, above average height for a Chinese, somewhat stooped, with a head of thick black hair grown very long, and with large, searching eyes, a high-bridged nose and prominent cheekbones." His first impression was of "an intellectual face of great shrewdness," reflecting Mao's vast understanding of human feelings, from the depths of physical suffering to the peaks of intellectual achievement.

In his lifetime, Mao has experienced all these emotions. Today he is portrayed as a national hero. His books on politics and even his poetry are treated as inspired works, so full of truth and guidance that the study of them will lead to miraculous transformations, whether it be in the raising of rice crops, the flying of airplanes, the behavior of children in schools, or the performance of the national basketball team. Yet once he was only the son of a Hunan rice merchant, a boy who worked with his father's hired laborer, who loved tramping through the countryside and meeting people, who toughened his body by walking shirtless through rain and sleet and by swimming in the coldest water he could find. Perhaps he had a premonition about the future.

Although he must be regarded as one of the outstanding figures in the whole of Chinese history, Mao has not been placed on a pedestal unapproachable by ordinary people. It is his belief that no gulf must be allowed to develop between

Plate 13. *Mao Tse-tung* (center) *with a group of Red Guards. Second from right is Chou-En-lai, and third from right is Lin Piao, Minister of Defense and Mao's chosen successor.*

the ruling class and the ruled. If it is, as it was under Chiang Kai-shek, China will never escape from the rigid system of privileges and taboos that prevented progress in the imperial age. This is why Mao remembers his lowly origins and continues to mix with the masses despite his image. This is why white-collar workers in Communist China, be they scientists, teachers, factory managers, or government officials, have sometimes had to spend some weeks each year working in the provinces, perhaps in the fields or factories. They have met people to whom they might otherwise never have spoken, shared their homes and food, and found out what life is like for them.

The peasantry has always formed the backbone of Mao's support. From time to time his policies have not found favor among educated Chinese, even among his Politburo colleagues. On such occasions, as when he advocated the hasty organization of communes* in 1958, he has toured the provinces himself, rallying support from those who have not been "contaminated" by wealth and power. No Chinese ruler has ever paid so much attention to the ordinary people, and they, flattered, have by their weight of numbers ensured his survival and that of his policies.

But popular enthusiasm does not mean that Mao's plans have always been the right ones. Chinese emperors of the past sometimes took notice of public opinion, but the wisest of them paid more attention to the advice of their ministers. In the last decade, Mao has neither agreed with nor trusted his "ministers." Indeed, most of them were dismissed and disgraced during the Cultural Revolution and their places taken by loyal Maoists. The latter may not prove to be the best men for their jobs, and the policy Mao expects them to continue even after his death—continuous purges and social upheaval to prevent the growth of capitalism—now seems hardly likely to be the best for China. Without Mao to inspire them in person, the Chinese people will perhaps be less ready to risk losing their few material possessions in another bout of fighting, looting, and anarchy such as accompanied the Cultural Revolution.

But in Shensi in 1936, the people had nothing to lose and everything to fight for, and Mao inspired them to fight. Edgar Snow was invited to visit the First Front Red Army defending the Soviet against the Nationalists to the north. The walk to the frontier, in southern Ninghsia, took a fortnight. It was

hard going. On the way he spent three days in a village called
Wu-ch'i Chen.

For hundreds of miles around there is only semipastoral country, the people live in cave houses exactly as did their ancestors
millenniums ago, many of the farmers still wear queues (pig-
tails) braided round their heads, and the horse, the ass, and the
camel are the last thing in communication. Rape oil is used for
lighting here, candles are a luxury, electricity is unknown, and
foreigners are as rare as Eskimos in Africa.

In this medieval world, it was astonishing suddenly to come
upon Soviet factories and find machines turning and workers
busily producing the goods and tools of a Red China.

Wu-ch'i Chen boasted the main Communist arsenal, located
in a mountainside.

Here I found over a hundred workers making hand grenades,
trench mortars, gunpowder, pistols, small shells and bullets, and
a few farming tools. A repair department was engaged in
rehabilitating stacks of broken rifles, machine guns, automatic
rifles, and submachine-guns. But the arsenal's output was crude
work, and most of its products equipped the Red partisans, the
regular Red forces being supplied almost entirely with guns and
munitions captured from enemy troops.

Much of the manufacturing machinery had also been captured, both here, where there were clothing and shoe factories, and in other industrial centers. Living and working
conditions were primitive but bearable, and food, wages, and
working hours were fairly distributed. Snow compared this
with what he had seen in Nationalist-run Shanghai:

I remembered . . . the hundreds of factories where little boy
and girl slave-workers sit or stand at their tasks twelve or thirteen hours a day and then drop, in exhausted sleep, to the dirty

cotton quilt, their bed, directly beneath their machine. I remembered little girls in silk filatures, and the pale young
women in cotton factories—all of them . . . literally sold into
these jobs as virtual slaves for four or five years, unable to
leave the heavily guarded, high-walled premises, day or night,
without special permission.

Edgar Snow stayed at the frontier through August and the
beginning of September. He was impressed with the discipline
of the Red Army. Never before had Chinese soldiers actually
earned respect for their good behavior and honesty. But then,
never before had they shared alike with their leaders, in good
times as in bad, in an egalitarian army.

After his return to Pao-an, Snow became apprehensive
about his line of retreat from Red China. Troops from
Nanking were replacing Tungpei soldiers along the Communist border. When he left the "capital" on October 20, only
one possible exit remained open, where the less vigilant Tungpei were still on duty. The following day he rumbled into
Sian on a truck. It was not a moment too soon, for on that
very night Nanking soldiers clamped down on all road movement around the city. There was panic for a while when
Snow discovered that his bag, containing precious notebooks
and rolls of film, had been thrown off the truck with weapons
for repair some twenty miles back, but they were recovered
in time, just before the blockade came down.[1]

---

[1] Edgar Snow wrote the story of his adventures in the Northwest Soviet
in a famous book, *Red Star over China* (Gollancz, rev. ed., 1968). The
quotations in this chapter are taken from it. In 1949 a popular revolution
swept the Communists into power over the whole country. The Chiang
Kai-shek regime was driven onto the island of Taiwan (Formosa),* where
it still is. Since then the contacts Snow made in 1936 have been renewed.
He is one of the very few American journalists to have interviewed the
Chinese leaders since relations between the two countries became strained.
The account of these meetings, and his impressions of China in 1960, are
told in *The Other Side of the River* (Gollancz, 1963).

Popular Entertainment in China

Since liberation,* changes have been taking place in the pattern of urban entertainment in China. The cinemas now show films made by the Chinese industry, which is an important one. Television networks are spreading. Before the Cultural Revolution, Western plays were being presented in the theaters, where the orchestra no longer sat on the stage and the audience no longer behaved as it did in pre-war China, or Tudor England. Symphony orchestras played Western classical music. Facilities for public sport had improved beyond all recognition, with special emphasis on the major national sports of basketball and table tennis.

However, reports from China in the summer of 1966 told about the cancellation of productions of Shakespeare, Molière, and other Western playwrights, and sports arenas now seem to be used as much for political demonstrations as for recreation.

Though China may again Westernize itself in some such respects, it will still maintain its traditional forms of entertainment. These include acrobatics, juggling, swordplay, puppetry, dance, and classical music. They are as popular today as they were in the Sung dynasty, or even the Han. As troupes go from village to village, helping to preserve folk arts and local traditions, they are received enthusiastically. The Chinese have a strong community spirit, and gathering to watch a live performance is better than sitting at home listening to the radio.

Two ancient forms of entertainment that in particular still draw crowds are the storyteller and the theater. The art of the public storyteller goes back at least as far as the Sung dynasty and probably much farther. The Sung performer specialized in one of four types of tale: adventure stories, Buddhist and supernatural stories, historical romances, and improvisation. As the use of printing spread he began to use prompt books, and these were later expanded into the first Chinese novels. They were the first works of literature to depart from the tight grammatical rules of earlier periods and to be written in everyday language. Today the storyteller is a popular entertainer, not only in the countryside but in the towns as well, where he can hold his own against the cinema and the theater.

In the theater, new plays mostly have political and revolutionary themes and are sometimes wholly propagandist in content. Critics of the Communist regime cite this as an example of the narrow attitude of the authorities toward the Arts. Yet even in its infancy, when Marco Polo was in China, the theater had a political flavor. Actors expressed their ill-feelings toward their Mongol overlords in unscripted lines and asides. The quality of the art was not debased then by involvement in politics. Neither does it necessarily follow that it is today.

Every age produces writers with new styles and interests. In its history the Chinese theater has seen many changes. Modern playwrights are doing no more than write about what interests them. Their subjects are not, as they usually were in the past, the doings of the upper classes but those of ordinary people. The theater-going public welcomes this, in the same way as Western filmgoers enjoyed the "kitchen-sink" dramas of the early 1960's. However, the government ensures that politics, i.e., praise for Communism and condemnation of Imperialism, are part and parcel of everybody's daily thinking, and this is reflected in the plays. The audience accepts this. So long as the spectacle is a good one, with colorful characters and plenty of action, it can swallow any amount of officially inspired clichés. For its part, the government welcomes the writers' new interest as a means of spreading its propaganda to a wider public. Edgar Snow went to an open-air theater in

Shensi, and saw how the Communists then mixed business with pleasure, indoctrination with entertainment.

The choice of contemporary themes has not meant that aesthetic values have suffered. Music, dancing, acrobatics, and swordplay are just as important as they were in the traditional theater. The outstanding new production of recent years, *The East is Red* (1964), has a cast of 3,000 and is a most colorful and dramatic experience.

Plate 14. A Scene from The East Is Red. *The middle banner reads "Long Live Chairman Mao."*

"Traditional" Peking theater, the style that evolved in northern China about the middle of the nineteenth century, is still a firm favorite. To the Western spectator it suggests a combination of theater, opera, and ballet, since it includes action, music, and dance.

Movement is fundamentally important, and to understand all its allusions requires considerable experience. It makes up for the lack of scenery, as for example when a group of actors sway in unison to suggest the rocking of a boat. It indicates emotions, as when an actor sweeps his right arm upwards to point at another's nose, showing anger. It indicates weather conditions, as when the actor's long sleeve is used like a fan to show great heat.

Movement must be graceful and must be performed in time with the music. This is difficult when the action is fast and swashbuckling and involves leaping and swinging swords or long poles. It can also be difficult when the actor himself is singing. Even such details as a switch in the direction of his gaze must be synchronized with the music.

The Chinese actor needs more specialized training in voice production than his Western counterpart. He must have a good singing voice as well as a strong speaking one. He must learn to laugh in highly conventionalized ways to indicate different emotions. Before 1912, women were not allowed on the Peking stage, so the actors who played the female roles had to have all these accomplishments in falsetto. This is not so today, but the training course is still arduous. At the Peking School of Dance it lasts seven years. In 1960 a visiting English correspondent, Felix Greene, was told that a dancer's education cost the state thirteen times more than that of an engineer.

All roles in the traditional theater fall into four categories, which are, in order of importance:

(1) *Sheng*   Male roles; may be either good or bad characters; no painted make-up; except for young men, all wear beards; examples of roles: officials, scholars, nobility, high-ranking soldiers, faithful retainers.

(2) *Tan*   Female impersonators; must convince the audience that they are feminine by their grace

and elegance and by exaggerating other female characteristics.

(3) *Ching*   More vigorous and dominating male roles;
               may be either good or bad; brightly painted
               make-up symbolizing strength, vitality, cun-
               ning; extremely powerful voice; examples of
               roles: outstanding statesmen, warriors, bandit
               chiefs.

(4) *Chou*   The clown; may be either male or female; the
               only category permitted to use everyday lan-
               guage and to make unscripted asides or topical
               jokes; always has a white patch around nose
               and eyes; examples of roles: peasants, minor
               officials, doorkeepers, mothers-in-law, female
               matchmakers.[1]

The essential thing about traditional Peking theater is that
it is not intended to be realistic. There is no scenery, only a
few simple props, which the actor uses to suggest the setting.
For example, he stands on a chair placed on a table at the back
of the stage to show that he is at the top of a mountain. If he
is a jailer, he may tilt a chair sideways on two legs to show
that he is opening the prison door to let somebody out. Cos-
tumes, make-up, movement, and voice production are all
stylized and quite unnatural. The plot itself may be unim-
portant and even trivial.

All this is because the object is not to tell a story but to
provide the actors with an opportunity to display their skills
and prowess. It is the collection of individual talents, working
in harmony, that determines whether a production is a good
one or not.

---

[1] Arranged marriages are illegal in Communist China.

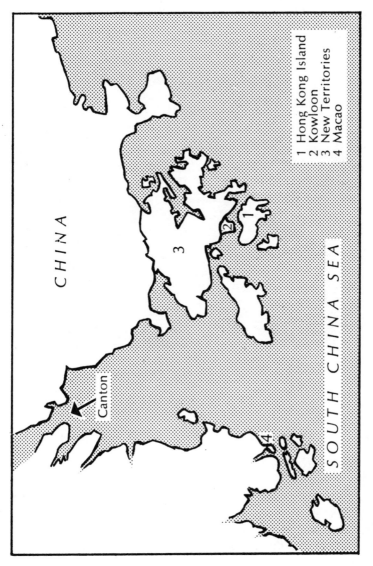

Map 7. Hong Kong

Plate 15. Hong Kong in 1966: Victoria, with Kowloon in the background

Further Reading

Edgar Snow has been called "the greatest reporter who ever came out of Asia." His major works on China have been mentioned in the footnote on p. 110 above. His autobiography, *Journey to the Beginning* (New York: Random, 1968), describes his meetings with not only the Chinese leaders but also such important world figures as Roosevelt, Gandhi, and Nehru.

A useful survey of twentieth-century Chinese history is G. Moseley, *China, Empire to People's Republic* (London: Batsford, 1968).

The illustrations in Robert C. North, *Chinese Communism* (New York: McGraw-Hill, 1966), a historical survey, are excellent. An up-to-date biography of Mao is Stuart Schram, *Mao Tse-tung* (Baltimore: Penguin, 1966).

One of the best pictures of life in Communist China before the Cultural Revolution is drawn by Felix Greene, *The Wall Has Two Sides* (London: Jonathan Cape, 1962), and a good introduction to Chinese geography for schools is K. Buchanan, *The Chinese People and the Chinese Earth* (London: Bell, 1966).

Appendixes

Comparative Chronological Chart 1

Chinese dynasty	Chinese history — Social and Political background	Chinese history — Notable events, innovations, etc.	Chinese dynasty	English ruling house, or dynasty	Western society and events
SHANG ?–1111 B.C.	Bronze Age. Beginning of political feudalism; administration well organized. Basically an agricultural civilization, but with some specialized industries and urban development. Writing perfected. Divination and superstition.	Bronze casting	SHANG		Dynasty XIX (1320–1200), the peak of Egyptian civilization
					Accession of Saul; David; Solomon
Spring and Autumn period 722–464	Decline of Chou central power; growth of independent feudal states. Decline in chivalric feudal obligations; rise of state consciousness and state patriotism		CHOU		Bronze casting perfected in Egypt
					Founding of Rome
	Iron Age				
Warring States period c. 460–221	Political theorizing; the wandering scholars. Known as the 'Period of the Philosophers'	Breast-strap harness			Est. of Roman Republic; Est. of Athenian Empire; Alexander the Great; Ptolemy I of Egypt
	Military cavalry				
CH'IN 221–206	Reunification by one state: first absolute administrative control over a large empire. Very harsh laws	Casting iron technique; Constitution of the Great Wall; Unification of writing systems	CH'IN		1st Punic War; 2nd Punic War, Hannibal crosses the Alps
Former, or Western Han	Harshness of Ch'in laws gradually relaxed. Good administration. Law code established for future dynasties. Civil Service examinations. Beginnings of state education. Prosperity of court, landowning and merchant classes. Trade with Rome.	Deep drilling; improvements in iron and steel technology; The first water-mills; Football	HAN	Romans come to Britain	Caesar's campaigns in Gaul; Roman civil wars
Usurper Wang Mang A.D. 9–23		Invention of paper			Life of Christ
Later, or Eastern Han		The first wheelbarrow; Use of stirrups; Paper manufacture; First use of tea; Collar harness; Use of coal			
THREE KINGDOMS 220–265			THREE KINGDOMS		
CHIN 265–420	Political disunion but a period of intellectual flourishing. Growth of Buddhism		CHIN	Romans evacuate Britain	Division of the Roman Empire; Sack of Rome by Alaric
DIVISION INTO NORTH AND SOUTH 420–589			DIVISION INTO NORTH AND SOUTH		Merovingian Empire; Breast-strap harness

Left-margin era spans: CHOU 1111–221; HAN 206 B.C. – A.D. 220

132

Chinese Dynasty	Description	Chinese developments	Dynasty	European rulers	European developments
SUI 589–618	Reunification	Cast-iron chain suspension bridges	SUI		Beginnings of feudalism. Use of stirrups. The Carolingian Empire. Charles the Great. Paper mill est. in Baghdad
TANG 618–907	A colourful period with high cultural attainments. China as the centre of a Pan-Asiatic atmosphere. Exchange of commodities and ideas. Beneficial effects on all levels of society. Apex of Buddhist influence	Earliest mechanical clocks. Block printing. Fleets of freshwater paddle-boats	TANG		Alfred the Great. Collar harness
FIVE DYNASTIES 907–960	Political disunion	Earliest printed books. Gunpowder	FIVE DYNASTIES		Earliest use of paper in Europe
SUNG 960–1279 / CHIN	Reunification. High standard of living. A period famous for its painting, porcelain and new interest in Confucian philosophy	Textile machinery. Bombs, grenades, flame-throwers. Movable type. Magnetic compass. Stern post rudder. Advances in theoretical and practical astronomy. Paper money. Barrel guns. Use of crank/connecting rod/piston rod. Blowing engine. Spinning-wheel	SUNG / CHIN	Normans	Crusades. Eleventh-century Renaissance. Deep drilling. Earliest paper manufacture. Magnetic compass. Wheelbarrow. Oxford University founded. Building of great European cathedrals
YUAN (MONGOL) 1279–1368	A conquering, non-Chinese dynasty employing non-Chinese officials. Free intercourse from the Atlantic to the Pacific	First Christian missionaries in China. Archbishopric of Peking established	YUAN	Plantagenets	Earliest mechanical clocks. The spinning-wheel. First mention of gunpowder. Barrel guns. Cast iron. Block, followed by movable-type printing
MING 1368–1644	Return of Chinese rulers. Science, industry and technology reach their highest point of development, but economy is still basically agricultural	Fleets of ironclad ships. Chinese navy the greatest in the world. Arrival of Jesuit scholars in Peking	MING	Lancaster and York / Tudors	Renaissance and Reformation. European university expansion in 14th–16th c. European voyages of discovery. Fall of Constantinople. Use of crank/connecting rod/piston rod. Decline of feudalism. First European paddle-boats. Thirty Years War. Louis XIV
CH'ING (MANCHU) 1644–1911	Non-Chinese, conquering dynasty. Reign of Emperor K'ang-hsi (1662–1722) an important period of art patronage. Exploitation of China by Western powers. Heavy financial losses. Crisis in confidence in Chinese civilization	Roman Catholic missionaries in China. Protestant missionaries active in 19th c. The Opium War. The T'ai P'ing Rebellion. The Boxer Rising	CH'ING	Stuarts / Hanoverians / Saxe-Coburg	Civil Service exams reach the West. Iron chain suspension bridges. The French Revolution. Industrial Revolution. European Iron Age
REPUBLIC 1911–1949	Political disunion. Severe social hardship. Awareness of the need to compete with the West. Traditional Chinese values decline	Rise of the Communist Party. Occupation by Japan in World War Two, followed by civil war (1946–49)	REPUBLIC		World War One. World War Two
COMMUNISM 1949–	Dramatic rise in national confidence. Reorganization of industrial and agricultural programmes aimed at raising basic standard of living	China becomes a nuclear power	COMMUNISM	Windsor	

Comparative Chronological Chart 2

Dynasty	Foreign thought	Chinese thought	Foreign literature	Chinese literature	Foreign painting	Chinese painting
SHANG ?–1111 B.C.			(20th c. B.C.) Egyptian Classical literature	Oracle bones	(15th c. B.C.) Egyptian tomb art	Decorative motifs on pottery and bronzes Calligraphy on shell, bone, bronze, etc.
			Early Psalms and Proverbs 2. Samuel			
CHOU			Homer Parts of Isaiah, Amos, Hosea	Parts of Shih Ching, Shu Ching, I Ching	Human figures on Greek pottery	
			Deuteronomy Jeremiah			
1111–221	Buddha	Confucius	Isaiah 40–55	First compilation of Lun Yü	Expert Greek vase painting of human and animal subjects	Painting and calligraphy on silk, wood, bamboo
	Sophism Socrates Plato Aristotle Epicurus	Mo Tzu Shang Yang	Sophocles, Herodotus, Euripides, Thucydides, Aristophanes, Xenophon			
		Chuang Tzu Meng Tzu Hsün Tzu Han Fei Tzu	Song of Songs Book of Daniel	Tso Chuan Kuo Yü		
CH'IN 221–206						
HAN 206 B.C.–A.D. 220	Christ St Paul	Confucianism emerges as the dominant court philosophy, but incorporates aspects of Legalism	Julius Caesar Cicero, Virgil, Ovid First Roman public library Pliny the Elder Tacitus	Shih Chi First Imperial library established, and a classified catalogue commissioned. Han Shu (first of the dynastic histories) Compilation of the Ch'u Tzu	Roman murals and mosaics Indian murals	Murals
			New Testament books			
THREE KINGDOMS 220–265						
CHIN 265–420	St Augustine of Hippo	Development of Buddhist thought in China	Civitas Dei	Short stories T'ao Yüan-ming (poet)	Zenith of Byzantine art	Ku K'ai-chih
DIVISION INTO NORTH AND SOUTH 420–589				Buddhist literature		Hsieh Ho

134

Period	Western thinkers	Chinese thought	Western literature	Chinese literature / learning	Western art	Chinese art
SUI 589–618	Mohammed		The Koran			Yen Li-pen (portraits)
T'ANG 618–907		Han Yü	*Beowulf*; Bede: *History of the English Church*	Public libraries; The great period of Chinese poetry: Li Po, Tu Fu, Po Chü-i		Wang Wei (the first landscapist) Han Kan (horses)
FIVE DYNASTIES 907–960			*Anglo-Saxon Chronicle*			Landscape artists: Li Ch'eng, Fan Kuan, Kuo Hsi, Mi Fu, Emp. Hui Tsung (birds and flowers), Mu Ch'i, Hsia Kuei, Ma Yuan, Chao Meng-fu, Ni Tsan
SUNG 960–1279	Thomas Aquinas	The reinterpretation of Confucian thought (neo-Confucianism): Ch'eng I, Chu Hsi	*Chanson de Roland*	Su Tung-p'o (poet); Compilation of collected works, encyclopedias, etc. reaches new intensity		
CHIN						Shen Chou Lü Chi (animals and flowers)
YUAN (MONGOL) 1279–1368			Dante; Chaucer; *Imitation of Christ*	The great age of Chinese drama. The beginnings of the Chinese novel	Leonardo da Vinci, Michelangelo, El Greco, Rubens, Rembrandt	Tung Ch'i-ch'ang
MING 1368–1644	Ignatius Loyola, Erasmus, St John of the Cross	Wang Yang-ming	Cervantes, Bacon, Shakespeare, English metaphysical poets, French dramatists, poets, prosodists, The beginnings of the European novel			Shih T'ao
CH'ING (MANCHU) 1644–1911	Leibniz, Pascal, Voltaire, Rousseau, Kant, J. S. Mill, Darwin, Marx	K'ang Yu-wei			Rococo art; Gainsborough, Goya, Constable, Turner	Kung Hsien
REPUBLIC 1911–1949		Mao Tse-tung: *Collected works*		The first literature written in the vernacular. The revolutionary writer Lu Hsün	Impressionism	
COMMUNISM 1949–		*Quotations from Chairman Mao*			Picasso	

The Traditional Rulers of China

P'AN KU	The first being in the Chinese creation myth; spent 18,000 years chiseling the earth out of chaos. When he died, the vermin on his body became the human race.
T'IEN HUANG, *Rulers of Heaven*	Thirteen brothers, each of whom lived for 18,000 years.
TI HUANG, *Rulers of Earth*	Eleven brothers.
JEN HUANG, *Rulers of Men*	Nine brothers. *The foregoing produced the earth in its present form.*
YÜ CH'AO SUI JEN	Thirteen families who taught men to make houses. Taught men to make fire and to calculate.

The Legendary Age of Five Rulers

(1) FU HSI (2953–2838[1])	The "founder of history"; taught fishing, animal husbandry, music, writing with symbols, marriage laws; reputedly the first emperor.
(2) SHEN NUNG (2838–2698)	The great agriculturalist; the "father of medicine."
(3) HUANG TI (2698–2598)	The "Yellow Emperor"; invented the calendar, wheeled vehicles, ships. His wife taught sericulture.
(4) YAO (2357–2258)	The first of the Perfect and Virtuous trio of rulers exalted by Confucius and Mencius. During his reign (2297 B.C.), there was a disastrous flooding of the Yellow River, which was brilliantly dealt with by Yü (*q.v.*).
(5) SHUN (2258–2208)	The second of the trio; not the hereditary successor of Yao, but nominated by him because of his extreme virtue; full of filial piety.*

The Hsia Dynasty

(The existence of this dynasty has not yet been established by archaeology.)

YÜ (2208–2177)	The third of the trio; again chosen for the throne because of virtue, not heredity; a very hard worker, just and well liked; the founder of the Hsia dynasty.

[1] Most dates are traditional and virtually meaningless.

CHIEH
(1818–1763)

The seventeenth ruler of the dynasty, known as "the tyrant." His extreme wickedness dried up rivers.

The Shang Dynasty

T'ANG
(1766–1753)

Defeated Chieh in 1766 B.C. and established the new dynasty; claimed to be descended from the Yellow Emperor.

P'AN KENG
(1400–1373)

Moved the Shang capital from Po, in eastern Honan, to Yin (Anyang). The date (1384 B.C.) has been verified by archaeologists. The Shang dynasty is sometimes known as the Shang-Yin, and sometimes simply as the Yin.

CHOU HSIN
(1153–1111)

Another tyrant. During his reign, the earl of the feudal state of Chou, whose name was Wen Wang, became very powerful.

The Chou Dynasty

WU WANG
(1111–1104)

The son of Wen Wang; defeated Chou Hsin in 1111[1] B.C.

CH'ENG WANG
(1104–1079)

A minor. The regency was excellently conducted for seven years by his uncle, the Duke of Chou (Chou Kung), who was the fourth son of Wen Wang. *Wen Wang, Wu Wang, and Chou Kung form another trio idealized by later political theoreticians.*

---

[1] Various proposals have been put forward concerning the date of the Chou conquest, ranging from 1122 B.C. and including 1111 B.C.

Sources of Chinese History

The Chinese have a special feeling for antiquity and the aged. In daily life this has been shown ever since the Shang dynasty by the important place occupied in the family by the grandparents or, if they are dead, by their memory and wishes. Their authority, and that of the father, has been strongly maintained, as we saw from Chang Hao's punishment of the boy convicted of unfilial behavior. This produced a respect that is still deeply ingrained. It has had its advantages, chief of which was the assistance it gave to the authorities in preserving law and order. It has also had disadvantages: Even today, the Hong Kong Government has difficulty moving some families from unsanitary hillside shacks to new resettlement apartments, simply because their grandparents lived there before them. To move, they say, would imply criticism of their standards.

More significant to us than Chinese family sentiments is the attitude toward the history of the country. Even in the Chou dynasty, there were some who were conscious and proud of a long continuity from what they regarded as a glorious past. This grew stronger as the centuries went by. It was justifiable, but it led in time to a fatal conservatism and self-satisfaction. The Confucian intellectuals who ran the empire dwelt in the past. They would allow no changes in government or industry that might endanger their hard-won position at the head of society. Private enterprise was carefully watched. Nationalization was one of the imperial governments' earliest weapons for preventing groups or individuals from becoming too powerful. Among the first industries to be controlled in this way were the Han salt and iron works. Another example was the silver industry in the sixteenth century. Private smelting and minting were prohibited, and mines were opened and closed at government direction as demand for the metal fluctuated. Nor were industrialists the only ones to suffer sanctions: We have seen what happened to the Buddhist Church in the ninth century.

The stifling of individualism became worse after the seventeenth century. Not only that, but the Chinese remained so unconvinced of their need for progress that, even before the Jesuits had gone, most of the valuable lessons they had once taught had been forgotten. For example, the official history of the Ming dynasty, published in 1750, declared that Holland might be near Portugal, which was near Malacca, but that Cheng Ho had sailed west seven times and had never seen it. Matteo Ricci might have wondered whether he had labored in vain.

When the power of the West was turned against China in the nineteenth century, it was forced to open its eyes. Had it not been for its conservative rulers, China might have welcomed the return of the foreigners, or at least have been adequately prepared to resist them. As it was, its complacent backwardness when confronted by the eager expansion of industrial Europe led to its collapse.

What had all this to do with the sources for Chinese history? Just this: Although the devotion to the past had disastrous political consequences in the nineteenth century, it had encouraged the careful treasuring of antiquities. In this respect, it was beneficial, because, of course, such things as pottery, bronzes, and paintings are firsthand evidence for the historian of how people lived in past ages.

Priceless private collections of treasures were handed down from one generation to another. Most are now to be found in the museums of China. The most famous of these are in Peking, but every large provincial town has its museum and almost every province its archaeological society. Important finds are frequently made, widening our knowledge of China's history. They are published in archaeological journals. It is not true to say that to the Communists everything before liberation "was evil and it is a virtue to be ignorant of it."[1]

Because the Chinese thought about historical continuity, they kept records. The oldest go back as far as the Shang dynasty, and they are continuous from the Han onward. Each dynasty wrote the history of its predecessor based on these records, arranging it under such headings as Major Events, Chronological Tables, Family Trees, and Monographs on subjects of political or economic importance. These works, known as the "official" or "dynasty" histories, provide a detailed and almost contemporary account of nearly 2,000 years of Chinese history. They present the official view of events. Very often their information can be supplemented from either general or specialized histories written by private individuals. These, too, were carefully preserved by later collectors and copyists. Finally, and providing local color, there exist thousands of handbooks compiled by the provincial authorities. The earliest of these date back to the Han. China has, in fact, the best collection of national and local historical records in the world.

---

[1] Professor Hugh Trevor-Roper in the *Sunday Times*, London, October 31, 1965.

Important Works of Early Chinese Literature

Analects, the

see *Lun Yü*.

Book of Changes

see *I Ching*.

Book of History
(or Documents)

see *Shu Ching*.

Book of Ritual
(or Etiquette)

see *Li Chi*.

Book of Songs
(or Poetry)

see *Shih Ching*.

Chan Kuo Ts'e
(Discourses of
the Warring
States)

A compilation of stories covering the period 453–209 B.C., made from sources in the Han imperial library by Liu Hsiang. The present work is a reconstruction by Sung scholars, "filling in" parts of the original, which had been lost.

Chou Li (Rites of Chou)	An early Han compilation purporting to describe the workings and ritual of the Chou administration in its heyday.
Ch'u Tzu	A collection of songs and poetry from the regions once covered by the state of Ch'u. It was put together in the second century A.D. and includes songs dating back to the fourth century B.C. The most famous of the collection is an allegorical epic, the *Li Sao*.
Chuang Tzu	A collection of Taoist writings, probably by a number of authors. One of these may have been Chuang Chou (?369–?286). Dates from the Warring States period.
Ch'un Ch'iu (Spring and Autumn Annals)	The records of the state of Lu, covering the period 722–464 B.C.
Chung Yung (Doctrine of the Mean)	Traditionally ascribed to the grandson of Confucius, Tzu Ssu (483–?402); actually compiled in the late Ch'in or early Han period. It is one of the chapters of the *Li Chi*, but has been published as a work in its own right since the Sung dynasty.
Erh Ya	An early glossary on words from the classics; also with some geographical material. Probably compiled in the third or second century B.C.

Han Fei Tzu	A legalist text, partly written by Han Fei Tzu (?–233 B.C.), partly by his disciples.
Hsiao Ching (Classic of Filial Piety)	Authorship unknown. The present version includes many quotations from earlier works and was made up for educational purposes, probably in the early Han.
Hsün Tzu	Mostly authentic material by the Confucian Hsün Tzu (*c.* 340–245 B.C.), with some additions by his disciples.
Huai Nan Tzu	A collection of Taoist essays from the court of the Prince of Huai-Nan, mid-second century B.C.
I Ching (Book of Changes)	A book of divination, perhaps from the Spring and Autumn period. Additions and commentaries, known as "wings," were added between late Chou and early Han times. These are concerned with the metaphysical implications of divination.
I Li	The remains of the early Han dynasty *Li Ching*, a handbook on ritual.
Ku Liang Chuan	One of three commentaries on the *Ch'un Ch'iu*.
Kuan Tzu	Reputedly by the seventh-century-B.C. politician Kuan Chung of Ch'i, but actually compiled about 300 B.C. Re-edited by

Liu Hsiang in the former Han dynasty. Its most important sections are on economics.

Kung Yang Chuan

One of three commentaries on the *Ch'un Ch'iu.*

Kuo Yü

A book of history covering much the same period as the *Tso Chuan;* once believed to be by the author of the *Tso,* though this is now discounted.

Lao Tzu (Tao Te Ching)

A basic text of Taoism and one of the great mystical works of world literature. Traditionally attributed to Lao Tan, a contemporary of Confucius, but probably later than the *Chuang Tzu,* i.e,. third century B.C. May be the work of a single author. A recent translation with a good introduction is by D. C. Lau (Baltimore: Penguin Classics, 1963).

Li Chi (Book of Ritual)

A late Chou or early Han work on etiquette, ceremonial, and customs.

Li Ching

see *I Li.*

Li Sao

see *Ch'u Tzu.*

Lieh Tzu

A Taoist text. It includes one chapter that supposedly represents the opinions of Yang Chu, a fourth-century-B.C. hedonist. The date of composition is disputed

but is probably later than that of the
Chuang Tzu.

Lü-shih Ch'un   Works of various Ch'in scholars, col-
Ch'iu   lected before 239 B.C. for the Ch'in Chan-
                      cellor, Lü Pu-wei.

Lun Yü   The reputed sayings of Confucius. Books
(The Analects)   3–9 of the total twenty are probably the
                      earliest, edited by his disciples. The pres-
                      ent collection, which includes chapters by
                      later Confucians, was selected from two
                      early Han versions later in the dynasty.

Mencius   see *Meng Tzu.*

Meng Tzu   Compiled during the Warring States pe-
                      riod by the disciples of Mencius (?372–
                      ?289). The book consists of reported
                      conversations between the teacher and his
                      contemporary heads of states.

Mo Tzu   The teachings of Mo Ti (*c.* 479–*c.* 381),
                      arranged with commentaries by his dis-
                      ciples. Warring States period.

Shang Chün Shu   The book attributed to Shang Yang, con-
                      taining details of his reforms. It may ac-
                      tually date from a hundred years after his
                      death in 338 B.C.

Shang Shu   see *Shu Ching.*

Shih Chi (Records of the Astrologer)	The first comprehensive history of China; written by Ssu-ma Ch'ien (?145–?90 B.C.), Grand Astrologer at the Han court. Its last authentic reference is to events in 100 B.C.
Shih Ching (Book of Songs, or Poetry)	Songs and verse handed down since early Chou times. The present selection of 300 songs was in existence in the time of Confucius, who used it for teaching purposes.
Shu Ching (or *Shang Shu*) (Book of History, or Documents)	A collection of historical documents. Parts may be eighth-century-B.C. and may have been used by Confucius as teaching material; most is a forgery of the third or fourth century A.D.
Shuo Wen	The first dictionary of the Chinese language; completed about A.D. 100 by Hsü Shen.
Spring and Autumn Annals	see *Ch'un Ch'iu*.
Ta Hsüeh	One of the chapters of the *Li Chi*, selected for it emphasis on the value of study and recognized as an independent work since the Sung dynasty. Traditionally attributed to Tzu Ssu or to the disciple of Confucius, Tseng Tzu; may actually date from as late as 200 B.C.
Tso Chuan	A history book covering roughly the same period as that of the *Ch'un Ch'iu*, i.e.,

eighth to fifth century B.C. It was edited from existing material and compiled with additions in the fourth century B.C. It is traditionally the most famous of the three commentaries on the *Ch'un Ch'iu*, but was not in fact intended as a commentary.

Dating and authorship: Modern editions of most of these books contain material incorporated over the centuries. Editors in the past were free to omit, change or insert passages according to what they believed to be the original author's intentions. Since they were not obliged to indicate their alterations, it is sometimes difficult to determine which is the basic text and which is later accumulation. Dates that have been ascribed in the past to the supposedly basic texts have generally been too early. Exact dating still awaits more detailed linguistic analysis.

On the authorship of pre-Ch'in texts, it is usually impossible to be specific. Most books contain differences in style that show them to be the writings of more than one person put together, probably by a later editor or copyist. The names of the authors were not considered important and were frequently lost.

The Confucian Classics

The following is a list of the classics that formed the canon of Confucianism. They were the standard texts used in colleges, schools, and homes to teach the Confucian approach to living. They covered, *inter alia*, government, rules of daily behavior, and the interpretation of history. The period in which they became part of the canon is shown in parentheses.

Known as "The Five Classics"
$\begin{cases} \textit{Shih Ching} \\ \textit{I Ching} \\ \textit{Shu Ching} \\ \textit{Ch'un Ch'iu} \\ \textit{Li Chi} \end{cases}$ (Han)

Kung Yang Chuan *Ku Liang Chuan* *Tso Chuan* *Lun Yü*	(becoming accepted as standard at the end of the Han)
Erh Ya *Hsiao Ching*	(T'ang)
Meng Tzu *Ta Hsüeh* *Chung Yung*	(Sung)

The *Lun Yü, Ta Hsüeh, Chung Yung,* and *Meng Tzu* were signaled out and grouped together by Chu Hsi in the thirteenth century. They have since been known as the 'Four Books' (*ssu shu* 四書).

The *Li Chi, I Li* and *Chou Li* are sometimes referred to as the 'Three Rituals' (*san li* 三禮).

Geography[1]

Area: 9,561,000 sq. km. (almost equal to that of Europe); cf.
U.S.A. 9,396,520 sq. km.; India, 2,947,420 sq. km.

Population: est. 800 million (more than one-quarter of the
world total); cf., India, 511 million + (1967); Europe,
452 million +; North America, 220 million +.

Population increase: est. 1.4–2% per annum, i.e., roughly 10–
15 million; cf., India, *c.* 2.5% per annum, i.e., 12 million +.

Population density: average 75 persons per sq. km. (ranging
from 440 per sq. km. in Kiangsu Province to 3 per sq. km.
in Sinkiang Province); cf., India, average 156 per sq. km.
600 million Chinese live southeast of a line Yunnan– Hei-
lungchiang. They occupy only one-sixth of the area of
the whole country. Urban population in 1956 was only
86 million, or 13%.

[1] Statistical information taken from unofficial Chinese sources and from
N. R. Chen, *Chinese Economic Statistics* (Edinburgh, 1967), *The United
Nations Statistical Yearbook, 1967* (published 1969), and *The United Nations Demographic Yearbook, 1968.* The latter estimate the total population
for the middle of 1967 as 720 million. The only official Chinese figures on
population are those revealed in 1953 by the first general census and in 1957
by partial registration data.

Largest cities: (1969 estimates)

    10 million + : Shanghai

     7 million + : Peking

     4 million + : Tientsin

     3 million + : Canton

     2 million + : Chungking, Shenyang (Mukden), Wuhan

     1 million + : Changchün, Chengchou, Chengtu, Fushun, Harbin, Luta (Dairen), Nanking, Sian, Taiyuan, Tsingtao.

Communications: Most cities are linked by rail and air, though not yet adequately. Direct air links with U.S.S.R., North Korea, Tokyo, Hanoi, Rangoon, Karachi, Paris, London.

Waterways: 60,000 miles of navigable waterways.

Natural resources: Oil, natural gas, uranium, coal, iron, and all other minerals, metallic and non-metallic. Abundant water for irrigation and hydroelectric power. Abundant manpower, and some land as yet undeveloped.

Main crops: Rice, wheat, cotton, millet, tea, kaoliang, livestock.

Crops with fast-rising output: Sugar, rubber, cocoa, timber.

Climate:—North: dry, very cold winters; wet, warm summers.

    —South: mild winters; very hot, wet summers. In the western provinces, rainfall is negligible for most of the year.

The Capitals of China

The cities listed are those that were the capitals for the greater part of each dynasty.

DYNASTY	CAPITAL
Shang (after 1384 B.C.)	Anyang
Western Chou	Hao, near Ch'ang-an
Eastern Chou	Loyang
Warring States period	no overall capital
Ch'in	Ch'ang-an
Former Han and Wang Mang	Ch'ang-an
Later Han	Loyang
Three Kingdoms	Loyang, Nanking, Chengtu
Northern Dynasties	Ch'ang-an
Southern Dynasties	Nanking
Sui	Ch'ang-an
T'ang	Ch'ang-an and Loyang
Five Dynasties	Kaifeng and Loyang
Sung	Kaifeng
Southern Sung	Hangchow
Yuan	Peking

DYNASTY	CAPITAL
Ming	Nanking and Peking
Ch'ing	Peking
Republic (1911–28)	Peking
Nationalist (1928–49)	Nanking
Communist	Peking

Chinese Names

In Chinese, the surname is written first. It is followed by the personal, or given name. If there are two given names, they are hyphenated: e.g., Tseng Kuo-fan; Li Hung-chang; Tso Tsung-t'ang. Sometimes the surname is double-barrelled: e.g. Ssu-ma Ch'ien; Ou-yang Hsiu. Chinese who have adopted Western customs sometimes write their given names before their surnames. Thousands of surnames are listed. Only about five hundred are in use today, and of these less than half are common.

Given names are chosen for the meaning of the characters used, which are often propitious or complimentary. Later in life a man might take or be given other names having associations with his career, his literary achievements, etc. He might also be given a new title posthumously.

The most famous philosophers of the Warring States period have the character 子 , *tzu*, added to their surnames: K'ung Tzu (Confucius), Meng Tzu (Mencius), Chuang Tzu, Mo Tzu, etc. This has traditionally been thought to be an honorific title, "Master," but there is actually some doubt as to its original implication.

The titles for emperors and empresses were also carefully chosen for their meaning and consisted of either two or three characters. Sometimes a title was chosen that had already been adopted by an emperor of an earlier dynasty. To avoid any possibility of confusion, therefore, the dynasty is often specified whenever an imperial title is mentioned, thus:

Han Wen-ti (179–156 B.C.)	Emperor Wen (the Cultured Emperor) of the Han dynasty.
Sui Wen-ti (A.D. 589–605)	Emperor Wen of the Sui dynasty.

Administration

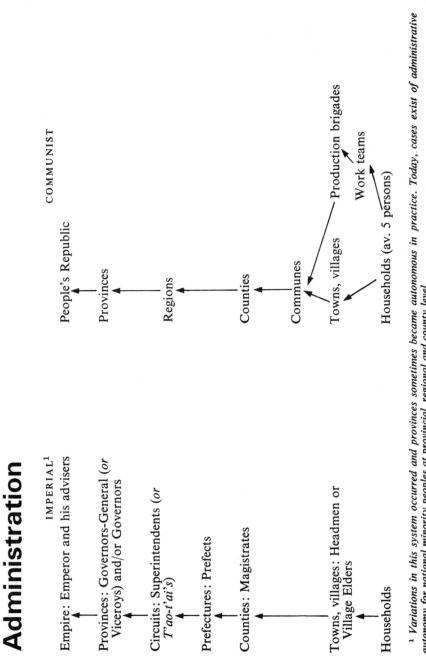

IMPERIAL[1]

Empire: Emperor and his advisers

Provinces: Governors-General (*or* Viceroys) and/or Governors

Circuits: Superintendents (*or* T'ao-t'ai's)

Prefectures: Prefects

Counties: Magistrates

Towns, villages: Headmen or Village Elders

Households

COMMUNIST

People's Republic

Provinces

Regions

Counties

Communes

Towns, villages

Households (av. 5 persons)

Production brigades

Work teams

[1] *Variations in this system occurred and provinces sometimes became autonomous in practice. Today, cases exist of administrative autonomy for national minority peoples at provincial, regional and county level.*

Glossary

Bactria	Corresponding approximately to modern Afghanistan.
Bamboo	A plant with many varieties, some of which grow to 40 ft. and have a diameter of 3 ft. It is used as a strong type of scaffolding.
Bastinado	Corporal punishment inflicted with a bamboo cane. In 156 B.C., the dimensions of the cane were fixed as: length 5 ft., thickness 1 in., tapering to ½ in.; all knots to be planed off.
Bodhisattva	One who has become enlightened but who has renounced his right to enter Nirvana and remained on earth to help less perfect men.

Buddha	One who has lifted himself out of the concerns of this world by self-denial and meditation and has entered Nirvana (eternal peace). The originator of the philosophy and first, or "historical" Buddha was Gautama, the son of an Indian prince (sixth–fifth century B.C.)
Buddhism	An Indian religion that took root in China and spread via Korea to Japan in the sixth century A.D. *See* Chapter 3.
Cathay	The medieval name of China. In 1605, Matteo Ricci showed for the first time that the China reached by sea in the sixteenth century was the same country as "Cathay," which earlier travelers had reached by an overland route.
Ch'ang-an	A former capital city, known as Sian or Sianfu since the Ming dynasty.
Chinese	A native of China is called a Chinese. To talk of a "Chinaman" is like talking of an "Englandman" or an "Americaman." Because it was a word commonly used by nineteenth-century Westerners, it is still associated by some Chinese with the imperialistic attitude and may cause offense.
Clan	An association of people living in the same area and possessing the same surname who believed that they had a common ancestor. The organization had strict rules for mutual assistance and protection

of its members. The clan leader, often a government officer, had considerable powers over members. Imperial clansmen were those who could trace their ancestry back to the founder of the dynasty.

Communes

Administrative units into which the country has been divided since 1958. Significant in organizing communal labor; distributing food; sharing tools, machinery, and raw materials; and promoting education, health facilities, and civil engineering schemes. They have not eliminated the desire for some private ownership and private enterprise, as Mao at first hoped they would. A more detailed description will be found in K. Buchanan, *op. cit.*

Confucianism

The philosophy based on the teachings of Confucius. The code of life for officials which dominated almost every aspect of life in China from the first century B.C. until the 1920's. *See* Chapter 3.

Corvée

Compulsory periods of work on tasks assigned by the authorities. Frequency and duration of these periods varied: The standard during the Han dynasty was one month per year.

Cultural Revolution

The most recent and extensive purge inspired by Mao Tse-tung to discredit anybody in a position of authority who could be suspected of turning toward capitalism. The teenage Red Guard movement was formed (August, 1966) to assist in the purge but became too destructive. Mao may have underestimated the strength of the "opposition." In the government, it developed into a power struggle in which Mao dismissed the President of the Republic, Liu Shao-ch'i. It destroyed the Communist Party and forced Mao to call upon the army to re-establish law and order. It encouraged fighting between groups and factions, even within the Red Guards and the army itself. It halted education for more than two years, destroyed China's growing reputation in the world, and left what may still be an anarchical situation in some provinces.

The Cultural Revolution began in 1965 and has not yet been formally concluded.

Dialects

Dialects in China are not variations on a standard tongue. They are different and mutually unintelligible spoken languages. The most widely used are Mandarin (over two-thirds of the country), Cantonese, Hakka, Hsiang, Wu, and the Min languages (all in the south and southeast).

Dynasty

A period of history during which the succession to the throne is retained by one family. In China the rule of primogeniture was often broken, and family feuds, intrigues and murders were common.

Emperor	Known as the "Son of Heaven," the go-between of heaven and earth. Responsible to heaven for his people's welfare: If they suffered, heaven showed its displeasure with earthquakes, floods, and droughts, and the people were then entitled to revolt and choose a new ruling house. Emperors might be dictators, but the Confucian system guarded against this by surrounding them with ministers to offer advice on matters of both detail and principle. The private lives and work of even the most senior ministers were themselves subject to investigation by other officials. Checks and balances were intended to prevent the misuse of power at all levels. In the Ming and Ch'ing governments there were six Boards, or Ministries: Home Affairs, Revenue, Ceremony, War, Punishments, and Public Works.
Eunuchs	Often placed in high court positions close to the emperor because they were thought to be safe from the normal temptations of family ambitions and intrigue with the royal concubines. Yet in the Han, T'ang, and Ming periods especially, they formed one of the powerful cliques that struggled with emperors for control of the government. Sometimes referred to as "ill-omened crows" or "palace rats."
Extraterritoriality	The principle whereby the citizens of one country resident in another are exempt

from its laws and subject only to their own. Although this is contrary to international law, twenty countries compelled China to accede to its practice, and abuse, on its territory between 1843 and 1943.

Ferghana

Corresponding approximately to modern Tadzhikistan, in the southern U.S.S.R.

Filial Piety

The respect and devotion of a son for his parents. Extended in Confucian usage to mean his duties to his clan, those of a citizen to his officials and of the officials to the emperor. The code of behavior was strictly enforced by heads of families.

Grand Canal

In China, the major rivers flow from west to east. The canal was built to link north and south. It was completed by Kublai Khan in 1283 and incorporated many earlier canals. The oldest section had been dug in the fifth century B.C. Length, Peking-Hangchow: 1,000-plus miles.

Great Wall

The longest man-made structure in the world. Built by connecting up existing walls between 220 and 210 B.C. Extended during the Han dynasty and mostly rebuilt under the Ming.
Length: (est.) 3,000 miles.
Height: (average from present remains) 21 ft. 8 in.
Width: (average from present remains) base 21 ft. 4 in.; top 18 ft.

Hong Kong

A British colony on the south coast of China and one of the most prosperous ports in the world. Pop. *c*. 4 million. Capital, Victoria. It consists of three parts (see map 7): (1) an island of 32 sq. miles, ceded to Great Britain in 1842; (2) the industrial city of Kowloon, on land ceded in 1860; (3) the New Territories: 360 sq. miles of the mainland behind Kowloon, and more than 200 islands. It includes towns and agricultural and fishing villages. On 99-year lease granted in 1898.

Huang Ho
(Yellow River)

Called "yellow" because of the vast amount of silt it carries. The bed of the river builds up rapidly, causing frequent and serious flooding: hence its nickname, "China's sorrow." Its valley through Shensi/Shansi and Honan is known as the "cradle of Chinese civilization," for it was here that the earliest Chinese lived. Length: *c*. 3,000 miles.

Imperial

The imperial era in China, i.e., the period of rule by emperors, lasted from the accession of the First (Ch'in) Emperor in 221 B.C. until the close of the Ch'ing dynasty in 1911.

Imperial
Academy

The first Chinese university, established in Ch'ang-an by Han Wu-ti in 124 B.C. Students were prepared for entry to the higher Civil Service, and the curriculum consisted mainly of Confucian texts. After setbacks during the reign of Han An-ti (A.D. 107–26), the number of students is said to have risen to 30,000 under his successor.

Imperial Maritime Customs Service

Established 1861 to collect import dues, etc., from the treaty ports. Senior staff were foreigners (700 in 1895), who proved themselves more efficient than the Chinese; Chinese and foreigners worked together in junior ranks. Collected one-third of total government revenue by 1898. After 1896, it also ran the first national Post Office.

Indemnity

Financial reparation for loss of life or damage caused by war, etc. During the nineteenth century, China contracted so many of these huge obligations to the Western Powers that it had to borrow the money to pay them from Western banks and governments themselves, at a rate of interest usually about 5%. China thus became enormously in debt.

Jade

A word used in Chinese to designate many precious stones, but properly meaning nephrite or jadeite. It is hard, has a smooth and beautiful texture when polished, is cold to the touch, and produces a musical note when struck. It comes in a wide range of colors.

Lacquer	The sap of the lacquer tree. It is treated to produce a hard, damp- and heat-resistant varnish. It can be stained or painted and makes an attractive, lustrous surface. Lacquer was used as a preservative as long ago as the Warring States period, and some objects have survived unspoiled in tombs for more than 2,000 years.
Li	About one-third of an English mile.
Li Pu	The Ministry of Home Affairs. *See* Emperor.
Liberation	The Chinese Communist term for the Revolution of 1949.
Loess	A fine yellow earth that covers northwest China in depths of up to 350 ft. Accumulated over millenniums from dust blown down from the Gobi Desert. Extremely fertile, even with low rainfall. Erosion produces many caves and strange shapes in the loess landscape.
Macao	A small Portuguese colony 40 miles west of Hong Kong. Occupied and administered by the Portuguese since 1557, but not ceded to them until 1887. Before the opening of Hong Kong as a colony, Macao was the center for Western merchants and missionaries wishing to make contact with the Chinese.

Mandarin (1) A general term used in the West for Chinese officials in the imperial era.
(2) A Western term for the most common dialect of the Chinese language. *See* Dialects.

Mourning By the rules of filial piety, three years' mourning followed the death of a man's father. During this time the son had to retire from public life, eat and dress plainly, and sacrifice to the departed spirit.

Opium A drug made from poppy seeds. It is smoked in a special pipe and is extremely habit-forming, leading to complete debility and death. The vice has now been wiped out in China, but it is serious in Hong Kong.
The first Anglo-Chinese war (1839–42) is usually called the "Opium War," but the real issue was the more general one of East-West relations.

Peking First made capital of China in 1271. "Peking" means "northern capital." From 1928 to 1949, the city reverted to its original Ming name, Peiping—"northern peace."

P'i p'a An instrument resembling a lute, with four or six strings.

Romanization The representation in Roman letters of the pronunciation of Chinese characters, e.g., Ch'ing (清), Ming (明), T'ang (唐).

Sanskrit	The major language of ancient India. It has a vast literature but is now spoken only by a small number of people.
Sinicize	To cause a non-Chinese to adopt Chinese customs, manners and behavior.
Sogdiana	Corresponding approximately to parts of modern Uzbekistan and Turkmenistan in the southern U.S.S.R. The capital was Maracanda (Samarkand).
Soviet	A district in China under Communist control between 1927 and 1937.
Taiwan (Formosa)	A large island off the southeast coast of China, formerly forming part of Fukien Province. Ruled by the Nationalist party under Chiang Kai-shek with American aid. It occupies the Chinese seat in the United Nations while the Peking government, representing over 800 million Chinese, goes unrecognized. Sometimes called "Free China."
Taoism	A Chinese philosophy dating from the Warring States period (*see* Chapter 3). A popular form developed known as "religious" Taoism, which encompassed many superstitious beliefs and practices.
Western Regions	The Tarim Basin dependencies in the Han dynasty.

Yangtze Kiang   One of the longest rivers in the world
(*c.* 3,500 miles). Known in China as the
Great River, and the stretches above
Szechwan Province as the Golden Sand
River. Navigable by ocean-going vessels
almost up to Szechwan. Its fertile valley
is sometimes referred to as the "rice bowl
of China." Nearly one-tenth of the
world's population lives there.

Yellow River   *See* Huang Ho.

Index